The Gambling Addiction

CLIENT WORKBOOK

2
EDITION

The Gambling Addiction

Addiction

CLIENT WORKBOOK

2

EDITION

ROBERT R. PERKINSON

Keystone Treatment Center,
Canton, South Dakota

Los Angeles | London | New Delhi
Singapore | Washington DC

Los Angeles | London | New Delhi
Singapore | Washington DC

FOR INFORMATION:

SAGE Publications, Inc.
2455 Teller Road
Thousand Oaks, California 91320
E-mail: order@sagepub.com

SAGE Publications Ltd.
1 Oliver's Yard
55 City Road
London EC1Y 1SP
United Kingdom

SAGE Publications India Pvt. Ltd.
B 1/I 1 Mohan Cooperative Industrial Area
Mathura Road, New Delhi 110 044
India

SAGE Publications Asia-Pacific Pte. Ltd.
33 Pekin Street #02-01
Far East Square
Singapore 048763

Acquisitions Editor: Kassie Graves
Editorial Assistant: Courtney Munz
Production Editor: Brittany Bauhaus
Copy Editor: Megan Markanich
Typesetter: C&M Digitals (P) Ltd.
Proofreader: Theresa Kay
Cover Designer: Bryan Fishman
Marketing Manager: Katharine Winter
Permissions Editor: Adele Hutchinson

11 12 13 14 15 10 9 8 7 6 5 4 3 2 1

Contents

Introduction   **1**
  Honesty   1
   Meetings   2
   Higher Power   2
   Gambling Patient Exercises   3
   Motivation   3

Gambling History   **7**

Honesty for Gamblers   **21**

Step One for Gamblers   **33**
  Powerlessness   34
  Unmanageability   41

Step Two for Gamblers   **53**
  A Power Greater Than Ourselves   58

Step Three for Gamblers   **65**
  The Moral Law   65
  The Key to Step Three   67
  How to Turn It Over   67

Step Four for Gamblers   **75**
  Personality Defects   78
  Physical Liabilities   80
  Time-Out   80
  The Way to Recovery   81
  We Stay on Track Through Action   82
  Physical Assets   83
  Mental Assets   85
  The Autobiography   91

Step Five for Gamblers   **93**

Relapse Prevention for Gamblers   **95**

Relapse Is a Process   95

The Relapse Warning Signs   95

Interpersonal Factors   95

When You Experience a Warning Sign   97

Positive Outcome Expectations   99

High-Risk Situations   100

How to See Through the First Bet   108

Lapse and Relapse   109

The Behavior Chain   110

How to Cope With Triggers   110

How to Cope With Craving   111

A Daily Relapse Prevention Plan   111

Social Support System   112

People Who Can Help You in Recovery   113

Personal Recovery Plan   **115**

Statement of Commitment   120

Stress Management   **123**

Relaxation   124

Day 1   126

Day 2   126

Day 3   126

Day 4   126

Day 5   126

Day 6   126

Day 7   127

Exercise   127

Exercise Program   128

Changing Your Lifestyle   128

Problem Solving Skills   128

Developing Pleasurable Activities   128

Social Skills   133

Appendix 1. Daily Craving Record   **137**

Appendix 2. Pressure Relief Group Meeting and Budget Form   **139**

To the Gamblers Anonymous Group   139

The Choice Is Yours   140

Directions   141

To the Creditor   141

Budget   142

List of Creditors   145

Repayment Schedule   146

Financial Summary   147

References   **149**

About the Author   **151**

Recovery Journal   **153**

Introduction

Congratulations and welcome to treatment! You have made a monumental step in recovery. You can be proud of yourself. You can feel confident that treatment works. Over 90% of patients who work this program stay clean. You will get your life back if you change a few simple things. These are called the tools of recovery. This program is not hard; it's easy, but you must do your part. It's going to take some work.

The illness of addiction is not you. You don't have to feel bad about yourself. This illness is a disease that lives inside of you. You are not bad; the illness is bad. You will find that this illness has a life of its own, and it will fight for survival. It will do everything in its power to get you off track and get you back to addictive behaviors. The illness is cunning, baffling, and powerful. It often works out of your awareness and you must substitute healthy thoughts and behaviors to stay in recovery.

Addiction is a chronic brain disease. The brain has been hijacked by an illness. You must be disciplined and fight for your life. Ninety-five percent of untreated addicts die of their addiction. Gamblers and their spouses have a much higher suicide rate. You are in a life and death struggle, and the war will be played out inside of your mind, body, and spirit. You are in for a fight for your life, but you are not alone. We are going to fight with you.

There are three things that you can do that will bring the illness under control. These new behaviors may seem unnatural for you at first, but you must do them all. If you leave one of the tools out, your chances of recovery significantly decrease.

Let's briefly go over the tools so that you can begin to understand them. You have to do three things to recover from pathological gambling: (1) get honest, (2) go to meetings, and (3) get on a spiritual journey to a Higher Power of your own understanding.

HONESTY

You have to get honest because the disease must lie to operate. The illness lives in and grows in the self-told lie. Addiction cannot survive in the light of the truth. You must try from the beginning to be honest with yourself and others. You don't have to tell everyone everything, but you have to stop telling lies. Gamblers take a game of chance and try to make it a game of skill. The gaming industry makes sure that all of their games are games of chance. That means you cannot by any means predict the outcome. Gamblers think the day, number, color, person, casino, machine, race track, or sports game can be predicted. This is a lie. Games of chance cannot be predicted. You need to stop lying to yourself and others and walk in the truth. You can't solve real problems with real people unless you have the facts. Treatment is a never-ending search for the truth.

Meetings

You have to go to recovery group meetings and help others there. Nothing protects you against relapse like helping other addicts. This works when all else fails. You will find out that you are uniquely skilled at helping other problem gamblers, and no one else will do but you. You are the only one who will be there at the right time, at the right place to share a truth that moves another addict toward recovery. You might not feel like helping others right now. You might just want to help yourself, but that's not going to work. This is a program of the *we*, not a program of the *I*. At the core of addiction is self-centeredness. We are going to get out of self and get into helping others. This will restore your sense of purpose and make you feel good about yourself again. The illness says you are worthless so you must prove it wrong. You can't be worthless and be helping others at the same time. These things are incompatible. By helping others, you will prove the illness is wrong. So even if it is not like you, even if you feel like you don't fit in, even if you feel uncomfortable in groups, you must begin encouraging others in recovery. All you have to do is share your experience, strength, and hope.

Higher Power

You have to get on a spiritual journey to a Higher Power of your own understanding. You don't have to be a religious person. This is a spiritual journey, not a religious one. All you have to do is be willing to seek a Higher Power of your own understanding. If you don't believe in God, that's fine; just be open-minded and willing. That's all you need to do.

Now that's simple, isn't it? Get honest, go to meetings, and get on a spiritual journey. You can do that. But remember that the illness is at work. The addict that lives inside of you is going to fight you every step of the way. That stinking thinking inside of your mind, body, and spirit is going to find reasons why you will not do each of these three things. It may say that if you tell people the whole truth about you they won't like you. It may say the meetings are boring and unnecessary. It may say that there is no Higher Power. The illness is going to fight for survival, and you must work hard to overcome it.

So that is the war. The battle lines are drawn. The enemy is confident of victory. You've tried to get clean and sober before, and you have always failed. The illness wants you to stay sick because it knows how important you are. It knows that if you get free then others will recover. Remember that you have an army on your side. You have a new family of brothers and sisters in recovery who understand you like no one else can. The staff knows how to fight this illness, and they know how to win. Get ready, prepare yourself, and be willing to go to any lengths. Follow this program, and recovery is right up ahead. Soon you will restore your life and be happy, joyous, and free.

Gambling Patient Exercises

These exercises have been designed to take you step-by-step through the recovery program. Complete each exercise *only* when your counselor says you are ready. Do not move ahead because you must practice and internalize the skills before you move on. Each exercise is a building block that leads to the next. If you move ahead too quickly, you will not receive maximum benefit. If you were going to build a house, you wouldn't begin by putting up the roof. You have to begin with the foundation. Once the foundation is carefully laid down, you can begin with the walls and finally the roof. So it is with recovery. Each step must be practiced and internalized before you move on to the next one. Your counselor may give you other exercises not in this book. These are for special problems that might make recovery more difficult for you. When you have completed an exercise, you will go over it in group or in a one-on-one session with your counselor.

When the group or counselor decides you have successfully completed the exercise, you will move on to the next one. There is no right way or wrong way to do these exercises; just do the best you can and remember that honesty is the foundation of recovery.

- Keep a journal of each day you are in treatment. What happened? What did you learn? What do you need to work on? As you journal, think about your recovery skills and how you need to use them.
- Tear out the Daily Craving Record from Appendix 1. Use as many sheets as you like, and make copies of more if you need them. Then rate your craving each day on a scale from 0 = no craving to 10 = severe craving. Then think of what happened to trigger your craving. Was it a thought, situation, feeling, person, place, or thing? Craving always follows thoughts.

"I can gamble if I want to."

"I can quit gambling on my own."

"I don't need treatment."

"I am not as bad as these people."

"I need money".

"The staff does not care about me."

"I have got to get out of here."

"I just got paid."

What were you thinking that caused you to crave? Throughout treatment, we are going to measure your thinking and behaviors. Then we are going to challenge your thoughts for accuracy. We are going to stop lying and live in the truth.

Motivation

Throughout treatment, you will find your motivation changing. Sometimes you will know you want to use, and sometimes you will know you want to get clean. At first you will be torn between gambling and your new life in recovery. This is good and normal. You need to process through all of the pros and cons of gambling. There are many reasons to continue using and many reasons to stop. Consider them all. If you want to stop gambling, you only need to do this for one day at a time. If you have decided to stay clean today, that's an incredible victory. The illness will not like it, but you have made your decision. You will make this decision every day until the choice becomes automatic.

Motivation is the conscious or unconscious stimulus that gives you the energy to act. You can have motivation to stay clean, and you can have motivation to return to your addiction at the same time. This is called ambivalence, and it feels uncomfortable. Once you have made your decision and begin working the program, you will feel more certain every day that you have made the right decision. In a few days, you will feel remarkably better. This is evidence that you are doing the right thing and you do not need gambling to be happy.

Prochaska and DiClemente proposed a model for motivation that goes through five stages of readiness for change. These stages are precontemplation, contemplation, preparation, action, and maintenance. Each stage characterizes a different level of motivational for change. If you move up one step in motivation, this is a treatment success. You might move up one or several steps, but remember if you are moving toward the truth you are in recovery (DiClemente, 2006; Prochaska, 2003; Prochaska & DiClemente, 1984).

- As you work through these exercises, you will learn about how the illness fooled you into thinking gambling was safe. As you uncover the truth about your disease, you will feel uncertain if gambling was good or bad. Carefully evaluating the pros and cons of your addiction will increase motivation by allowing you to explore your life and how it will differ if you change. For example, people who are in the precontemplative stage have no interest in changing. They know that gambling is good. But once you see the good things and the bad things about gambling, your motivation changes. Yes, gambling was good some of the time, but sometimes it was very bad. As you explore the pros and cons of the addictive behavior, you will become more willing to think about the positive aspects of changing.
- Once you process the good and bad things about gambling, you are in contemplation, where you work through the positive and negative aspects of gambling. Once the decision is made to try to stop the addiction then you must concentrate on what thoughts and behaviors need to change.
- That is preparation, where you plan the changes that will get you clean and help you stay clean. This might mean coming into treatment, going to 12-step meetings, talking with your family, or seeing your doctor.
- When you begin to do the things you need to do to stay clean and sober, this is the action phase. This is where you mentally, physically, and spiritually change the thoughts and behaviors that cause the addiction.
- Once the addiction stops then you will need lifelong skills to stay clean and sober. This is the stage of maintenance.
- You can be proud of yourself now because you have done something right. For a long time, you have been living a life full of pain and lies. Now you will step out

in truth to help yourself and others. This treatment is not just about you; it's about helping other addicts. The best thing you can do for yourself is to help somebody else. Remember this when you are feeling bad. When this happens, go to a 12-step meeting, call someone in the program, or find someone else in treatment and ask them how they are doing. Tell them your story, and give them an opportunity to tell their story. There is nothing more powerful than your story: how it was, what happened, and how it is now. Know that the second you stopped the addictive behavior that your brain started healing. You are healing as you read these words, and every day it gets better.

As you work through the exercises, stop occasionally and think about where you are in the stages of motivation for change. Check the box that marks your stage of motivation now.

I am in the _____.

_____ Precontemplation stage

_____ Contemplation stage

_____ Preparation stage

_____ Action stage

_____ Maintenance stage

Gambling History

This exercise will help you to become more aware of how gambling has affected your life and the lives of those around you. Answer the questions as completely as you can. It is time to get completely honest with yourself. Write down exactly what happened.

1. How old were you when you first gambled? Describe what happened and how you felt.

    _____

    _____

    _____

    _____

    _____

2. List all of the types of gambling you have ever participated in and the age at which you first gambled.

    Video Lottery

    Blackjack

    Bingo

    Scratch Tickets

    Poker (Cards)

    Horse Racing

    Slot Machines

    Powerball

    Sports Betting

    Pull Tabs

    Dog Racing

    Other

3. What are your gambling habits? Where do you gamble? With whom? Under what circumstances?

_____

_____

_____

_____

_____

4. Was there ever a period in your life when you gambled too much? Explain.

_____

_____

_____

_____

_____

5. Has using gambling ever caused a problem for you? Describe the problem or problems.

_____

_____

_____

_____

_____

_____

6. When you were gambling, did you find that you gambled more or for a longer period of time than you had originally intended? Give some examples.

_____

_____

_____

_____

_____

7. Do you have to gamble more now to get the same effect you want? How much more than when you first started?

_____

_____

_____

_____

_____

8. Did you ever try to cut down on your gambling? Why did you try to cut down, and what happened to your attempt?

_____

_____

_____

_____

_____

9. What did you do to cut down? Did you change the time, place, or game? Limit the amount ("I'll only spend $20 tonight")? Restrict your gambling to a certain time of day ("I'll only gamble after work")?

_____

_____

_____

_____

10. Did you ever stop completely? What happened? Why did you start again?

_____

_____

_____

_____

11. Did you spend a lot of time getting over your losses?

_____

_____

_____

_____

12. Were you ever obsessed with gambling that you had problems doing something dangerous such as driving a car? Give some examples.

_____

_____

_____

_____

_____

13. Did you ever gamble so much that you missed work or school? Give some examples.

_____

_____

_____

_____

14. Did you ever miss family events or recreation because you were gambling? Give a few examples.

_____

_____

_____

_____

15. Did your gambling ever cause family problems? Give some examples.

_____

_____

_____

_____

16. Did you ever feel annoyed when someone talked to you about your gambling? Who was this person, and what did he or she say? Give some examples.

_____

_____

_____

_____

_____

17. Did you ever feel bad or guilty about your gambling? Give some examples.

_____

_____

_____

_____

_____

18. Did gambling ever cause you any psychological problems such as being depressed or anxious? Explain what happened.

_____

_____

_____

_____

19. Did gambling ever cause you any physical problems or make a physical problem worse? Give a few examples.

_____

_____

_____

_____

_____

20. Did you ever lose track of time when gambling? Give some examples.

_____

_____

_____

_____

21. Did you ever get sick because you were gambling? Give some examples.

_____

_____

_____

_____

22. Did you ever have intense guilt because of gambling? Give some examples about how you felt.

_____

_____

_____

_____

23. Did you ever get nervous or suffer withdrawal symptoms when you quit gambling? Describe what happened to you when you stopped gambling.

_____

_____

_____

_____

_____

24. Did you ever gamble to avoid symptoms of withdrawal? Give some examples of when you used gambling to control withdrawal symptoms.

_____

_____

_____

_____

25. Have you ever sought help for your gambling problem? When? Who did you see? Did the treatment help you? How?

_____

_____

_____

_____

_____

26. Why do you continue to gamble? Give five reasons.

    1. _____

    2. _____

    3. _____

    4. _____

    5. _____

27. Why do you want to stop gambling? Give 10 reasons.

    1. _____

    2. _____

    3. _____

    4. _____

    5. _____

    6. _____

    7. _____

    8. _____

    9. _____

   10. _____

28. Has gambling ever affected your reputation? Describe what happened and how you felt.

_____

_____

_____

_____

_____

29. Describe the feelings of guilt you have about your gambling. How do you feel about yourself?

_____

_____

_____

_____

30. How has gambling affected you financially? Give a few examples of how you wasted money in your addiction.

_____

_____

_____

_____

31. Has your ambition decreased due to your gambling? Give an example.

_____

_____

_____

_____

32. Has your addiction changed how you feel about yourself?

_____

_____

_____

_____

_____

33. Are you as self-confident as you were before?

_____

_____

_____

_____

_____

34. Describe the reasons why you want treatment now.

_____

_____

_____

_____

35. List all of the types of gambling you have been involved in, in the past 6 months.

_____

_____

_____

_____

_____

36. List how often and in what amounts you have gambled in the past 6 months.

_____

_____

_____

_____

_____

37. List the life events that have been affected by your gambling (e.g., school, marriage, job, children).

_____

_____

_____

_____

38. Have you ever had legal problems because of your gambling? List each problem.

_____

_____

_____

_____

_____

39. Have you ever lost a job because of your gambling? Describe what happened.

_____

_____

_____

_____

_____

40. Do you want treatment for your gambling problem? List a few reasons why.

I am in the _____.

_____

_____

_____

_____

_____

_____ Precontemplation stage

_____ Contemplation stage

_____ Preparation stage

_____ Action stage

_____ Maintenance stage

Honesty for Gamblers

This is an exercise to help you get honest with yourself. In recovery, it is essential to tell the truth. As you will hear at every Gamblers Anonymous (GA) meeting, this is a program of rigorous honesty. Those who do not recover are people who cannot—or will not—completely give themselves to this simple program.

Dishonesty to self and others distorts reality. You never will solve problems if you lie. You need to live in the facts. You must commit yourself to reality. This means accepting everything that is real.

Gamblers lie to themselves when they think they can beat a game of chance. Chance means you cannot manipulate the outcome of a game. Gamblers constantly think they can figure a game out, which machine will win, which numbers will come up, which horse will win, which card they will draw or which number will come up in roulette or bingo. The actual odds are this: The house gets 6% of every dollar you bet, so if you continue to gamble you will lose every penny you have. Gambling establishments are not fancy because of the winners; they are fancy because they can predict that the odds are always in their favor. The casino will always win. All of the games are stacked in their favor, and there is no way you can predict a game of chance. Each time you play each game the odds are exactly the same. There is no way to predict which horse, number, color, or machine will win. The odds are exactly the same each time you play. Gamblers constantly think they can figure a game out and increase the odds of winning, but this is never true. Memorize this sentence, and say it over and over to yourself: If I continue to gamble, there is a 100% chance that I will lose everything.

A video lottery machine has a random number generator that randomly generates the next numbers. Let us say the odds on one machine are 4,000 to 1 big win. So imagine that you have 4,000 white marbles in a bin and 1 red marble. You spin the bin and draw out one marble. The odds of choosing the red marble are 4,000 to 1. Now you put the marble back in the bin, spin the bin, and draw out a marble. The odds are exactly the same 4,000 to 1. All gambling is a game of chance, and there is no way to predict when the machine, game, or player is going to change the odds. In the marble game, there will always be a 4,000 to 1 chance that you will win. The real odds are if you continue to gamble you will be penniless. A casino only offers games of chance—never games of skill. The house would not let you play a game of skill because you could learn the skill and increase your odds of winning. The house never makes this mistake. The odds are always in favor of the casino. If you continue to gamble, the casino will always win. If you continue to gamble, you will always lose everything.

Here is a list of 10 statements you may have said to yourself that gave you the illusion that you could figure out a game of chance.

1. This machine has not paid out all day; it is ready to pay. No, the odds are always the same.

2. This horse always wins on a muddy track. No, the odds of one horse winning are always the same.

3. This blackjack dealer is unlucky; this is the table to play. I would win here. No, with every deal the odds are always the same.

4. If I keep playing this color it has to win soon. No, the odds are always random.

5. This roulette dealer spins too fast, the ball runs too fast, and this makes it more likely that the ball will fall on number 22. No, the odds are random and always the same. If you continue to gamble, you will lose everything.

6. If I keep count of the numbers, I can figure this game out and increase my odds of winning. No, games of chance are not games of skill. The odds are the same every time you play the game.

7. I always use this machine. It pays out the best. No, a machine has a random number generator, and each time you play you have the same odds of winning.

8. If I keep playing the numbers of my birthday, I will win every time. No, the odds are if you continue to gamble you will lose every cent you have.

9. If I do not want to win, I win every time. No, the odds are always the same.

10. This is my lucky day. I cannot lose. No, the odds are random; you cannot predict or use a skill to change the odds at a game of chance.

People who are pathological gamblers think that they cannot tell the truth. They believe that if they do then they will be rejected. The facts, however, are exactly the opposite. Unless you tell the truth, no one can accept you. People have to know you to accept you. If you keep secrets, then you never will feel known or loved. You are only as sick as your secrets. If you keep secrets from people, then you never will be close to them.

You cannot be a practicing gambling addict without lying to yourself. You must lie—and believe the lies—or else the illness cannot operate. All of the lies are attempts to protect you from the truth. If you had known the truth, then you would have known that you were sick and needed treatment. This would have been frightening, so you kept the truth from yourself and from others. Let us face it. When we were gambling, we were not honest with ourselves.

There are many ways in which you lied to yourself. This exercise will teach you exactly how you distorted reality, and it will start you toward a program of honesty. Respond to each of the following as completely as you can.

1. *Denying:* You tell yourself or others, "I do not have a problem." Write down at least five examples of when you used this technique to avoid dealing with the truth.

    1. _____

    2. _____

    3. _____

4. _____

5. _____

2. *Minimizing:* You make the problem smaller than it really is. You may have told yourself, or someone else, that your problem was not that bad. You may have told someone that you lost a little money when, in fact, you lost a lot. Write down five examples of when you distorted reality by making the problem seem smaller than it actually was.

    1. _____

    2. _____

    3. _____

    4. _____

    5. _____

3. *Being hostile:* You get angry, shut people out, or make threats when someone confronts you about your gambling. Give five examples of when you expressed such hostility.

    1. _____

    2. _____

    3. _____

    4. _____

    5. _____

4. *Rationalizing:* You make an excuse. "I had a hard day." "Things are bad." "My relationship is bad." "My financial situation is bad." "The only way I can recover my losses is to gamble." Give five examples of when you thought that you had a good reason to gamble.

    1. _____

    2. _____

3. _____

4. _____

5. _____

5. *Blaming:* You shift the responsibility to someone else. "The police were out to get me." "My wife is overreacting." "My boss is a pain." Give five examples of when you blamed someone else for a problem that you caused by gambling.

1. _____

2. _____

3. _____

4. _____

5. _____

6. *Intellectualizing:* You overanalyze and overthink to excess about a problem. You avoid doing something about it. "Sure I gamble some, but everyone I know gambles." "I read this article that said this is a gambling culture." "I know this machine is ready to pay out." Give five examples of how you use intellectual data and statistics to justify your gambling.

1. _____

2. _____

3. _____

4. _____

5. _____

7. *Diverting:* You bring up another topic of conversation to avoid being confronted with your gambling. Give five examples.

1. _____

2. _____

3. _____

4. _____

5. _____

8. Make a list of five lies about your gambling problem that you told to someone close to you.

1. _____

2. _____

3. _____

4. _____

5. _____

9. Make a list of five lies about your gambling problem that you told to yourself.

1. _____

2. _____

3. _____

4. _____

5. _____

10. Make a list of 10 people to whom you have lied.

1. _____

2. _____

3. _____

4. _____

5. _____

6. _____

7. _____

8. _____

9. _____

10. _____

11. How do you feel about your lying? Describe how you feel about yourself when you lie.

_____

_____

_____

_____

_____

12. List five things you think will change in your life if you stop gambling and tell the truth.

_____

_____

_____

_____

_____

13. How do you use lies in other areas of your life?

14. When are you the most likely to lie? Is it when you have been gambling?

15. Why do you lie? What does it get you? Give five reasons.

1. _____

2. _____

3. _____

4. _____

5. _____

16. Common lies of gamblers are listed here. Give a personal example of each.

   A. Breaking promises:

_____

_____

_____

B. Pretending you have not gambled when, in fact, you have:

_____

_____

_____

_____

_____

C. Pretending that you remember how long you had been gambling when, in fact, you lost all track of time:

_____

_____

_____

_____

_____

D. Telling someone that you gamble no more than others do:

_____

_____

_____

_____

_____

E. Telling yourself that you were in control of your gambling:

_____

_____

_____

_____

F. Telling someone that you rarely gamble:

_____

_____

_____

_____

_____

G. Hiding your gambling:

_____

_____

_____

_____

_____

H. Hiding money for gambling:

_____

_____

_____

_____

_____

I. Substituting gambling for other activities and then telling someone that you were not interested in doing what that person wanted to do:

_____

_____

_____

_____

J. Saying that you were too sick to do something when, in fact, you really wanted to gamble:

_____

_____

_____

_____

K. Pretending not to care about your gambling problem:

_____

_____

_____

_____

_____

People who are pathological gamblers lie to avoid facing the pain of the truth. Lying makes them feel more comfortable, but in the end they end up feeling isolated and alone. Recovery demands living in the truth. "I am a pathological gambler." "My life is unmanageable." "I am powerless over gambling." "I need help." "I cannot do this alone." All of these are honest statements from someone who is living in reality.

You can either get real and live in the real world or live in a fantasy world of your own creation. If you get honest, then you will begin to solve real problems. You will be accepted for who you are.

Wake up tomorrow morning, and promise yourself that you are going to be honest all day. Write down in a diary when you are tempted to lie. Watch your emotions when you lie. How does it feel? How do you feel about yourself? Write it all down. Keep a diary for 5 days, and then share it with your group. Tell the group members how it feels to be honest.

Take a piece of paper and write the word *truth* on it; then tape it to your bathroom mirror. Commit yourself to rigorous honesty. You deserve to live a life filled with love and truth. You never need to lie again.

List 10 reasons you want to stop gambling.

1. _____

2. _____

3. _____

4. _____

5. _____

6. _____

7. _____

8. _____

9. _____

10. _____

I am in the _____.

_____ Precontemplation stage

_____ Contemplation stage

_____ Preparation stage

_____ Action stage

_____ Maintenance stage

Step One for Gamblers

We admitted we were powerless over gambling—that our lives had become unmanageable.

—Gamblers Anonymous (GA) (1989b, p. 38)

Before beginning this exercise, please read Step One in *G.A.: A New Beginning* (GA, 1989b).

No one likes to admit defeat. Our minds rebel at the very thought that we have lost control. We are big, strong, intelligent, and capable. How can it be that we are powerless? How can our lives be unmanageable? This exercise will help you to sort through your life and to make some important decisions. Answer as completely as you can each question that applies to you. This is an opportunity for you to get accurate. You need to see the truth about yourself.

Let us pretend for a moment that you are the commander in a nuclear missile silo. You are in charge of a bomb. If you think about it, this is exactly the kind of control that you want over your life. You want to be in control of your thinking, feeling, and behavior. You want to be in control all of the time, not just some of the time. If you do something by accident or if you do something foolishly, then you might kill many people.

What is the first thing a compulsive gambler ought to do in order to stop gambling? The compulsive gambler needs to accept the fact that he or she is in the grip of a progressive illness and has a desire to get well. (GA, 1989a, p. 8)

To accept powerlessness and unmanageability, a gambler must look at the truth. People who are powerless over gambling do things that are harmful to themselves and others. They do most anything to stay in action—to keep gambling. Gamblers do not consider the consequences of their behavior, and they keep gambling until they are on the verge of death.

Gamblers are *in action* when they plan a bet, make a bet, or wait for a bet to come in. Once the bet is in, they are out of action. Being in action is a primary goal of compulsive gamblers. By staying in action, gamblers feel how they want to feel. They escape reality. They live in a fantasy world of their own creation. Some gamblers gamble for the thrill and some to escape. Now it is time to get honest with yourself.

POWERLESSNESS

People who are powerless do things that they feel bad or guilty about later. To gamble, they may lie, cheat, steal, hurt their family members, or do poor work. Make a list of five things that made you feel the most uncomfortable about gambling in the past.

1. _____

2. _____

3. _____

4. _____

5. _____

People who are powerless gradually lose respect for themselves. They will have difficulty in trusting themselves. List five ways have you lost respect for yourself due to gambling.

1. _____

2. _____

3. _____

4. _____

5. _____

People who are powerless will do things that they do not remember doing. When gamblers gamble, they can lose all track of time. They might think that they have been gambling for only a few minutes when, in fact, they have been gambling for many hours. If you gamble enough, you cannot remember things properly.
Describe five situations when you lost track of time while you were gambling.

1. _____

2. _____

3. _____

4. _____

5. _____

People who are powerless cannot keep promises they make to themselves or others. They promise that they will cut down on their gambling, and they do not. They promise that they will not gamble, and they do. They promise to be home, to be at work, to be at the Cub Scout meeting, or to go to school, but they do not make it. They cannot always do what they want to do. They disappoint themselves, and they lose trust in themselves. Other people lose trust in them. Gamblers can count on themselves some of the time, but they cannot count on themselves all of the time.

1. List five times you promised yourself that you would cut down on your gambling.

   1. _____

   2. _____

   3. _____

   4. _____

   5. _____

2. What happened to each of these promises?

   _____

   _____

   _____

   _____

   _____

3. Did you ever promise yourself that you would quit entirely?

   Yes   No

4. What happened to your promise?

   _____

   _____

_____

_____

_____

_____

5. Did you ever make a promise to someone that you did not keep because you were gambling? Give five examples.

   1. _____

   2. _____

   3. _____

   4. _____

   5. _____

6. Are you reliable when you are gambling?

   Yes   No

People who are powerless lose control of their behavior. They do things that they would not normally do when not in action. They might get into fights. They might yell at people they love—their spouses, children, parents, or friends. They might say things that they do not mean.

Have you ever gotten into an argument with someone because you were gambling? Describe five times.

   1. _____

   2. _____

   3. _____

   4. _____

   5. _____

The desire to gamble is very powerful. It makes a gambler feel irritable and impatient. People who are powerless say things that they do not mean. They say things that they feel guilty about later. We might not remember everything we said, but the other person does remember. List five times when you said something or did something that you did not mean when gambling or craving gambling. What did you say? What did you do?

1. _____

2. _____

3. _____

4. _____

5. _____

People are powerless when they cannot deal with their feelings. They may gamble because they feel frightened, angry, or sad. They medicate their feelings with gambling.

1. Have you ever gambled to cover up your feelings? Give three examples.

   1. _____

   2. _____

   3. _____

2. List the feelings that you have difficulty dealing with.

_____

_____

_____

_____

_____

_____

People are powerless when they are not safe. What convinces you that you no longer can gamble safely?

_____

_____

_____

_____

People are powerless when they know that they should do something, but they can-not make themselves do it. They might make a great effort to do the right thing, but they keep doing the wrong thing.

1. Could you cut down on your gambling every time you wanted for as long as you wanted?

   Yes   No

2. Did gambling ever keep you from doing something at home that you thought you should do? Give five examples.

   _____

   _____

   _____

   _____

   _____

3. Did gambling ever keep you from going to work? Give five examples.

   1. _____

   2. _____

3. _____

4. _____

5. _____

4. Did you ever lose a job because of your gambling? Write down what happened.

_____

_____

_____

_____

_____

People are powerless when other people have to warn them that they are in trouble. You may have felt as though you were fine, but people close to you noticed that something was wrong. It probably was difficult for them to define just what was wrong, but they worried about you. It is difficult to confront people when they are wrong, so most people avoid the problem until they cannot stand the behavior anymore. When gamblers are confronted with their behavior, they feel annoyed and irritated. They want to be left alone with the lies that they are telling themselves. Has anyone ever talked to you about your gambling? Who was this? How did you feel?

_____

_____

_____

_____

_____

People are powerless when they do not know the truth about themselves. Gamblers lie to themselves about how much they are gambling. They lie to themselves about how often they gamble. They lie to themselves about the amount of money they are losing—even when the losses are obvious. They blame others for their problems. Some common lies that they tell themselves include the following:

"I can quit anytime I want to."

"I only gamble a little."

"The police are out to get me."

"I only gamble when I want to."

"Everybody does it."

"I gamble, but I do not have a problem."

"Anybody can have financial problems."

"My friends will not like me if I do not gamble."

"I never have problems when I gamble."

"I can pay the money back later."

"From now on, I would just gamble a little."

"When I win, I am going to buy a present for my family."

Gamblers continue to lie to themselves to the very end. They hold on to their delusional thinking, and they believe that their lies are the truth. They deliberately lie to those close to them. They hide their gambling. They make their problems seem smaller than they actually are. They make excuses for why they are gambling. They refuse to see the truth.

1. Have you ever lied to yourself about your gambling? List five lies that you told yourself.

   1. _____

   2. _____

   3. _____

   4. _____

   5. _____

2. List five ways in which you tried to convince yourself that you did not have a problem.

   1. _____

   2. _____

3. _____

4. _____

5. _____

3. List five ways in which you tried to convince others that you did not have a problem.

1. _____

2. _____

3. _____

4. _____

5. _____

Therefore, it is not surprising that our gambling careers have been characterized by countless vain attempts to prove we could gamble like other people. The idea that somehow, some day, we will control our gambling is the great obsession of every compulsive gambler. The persistence of this illusion is astonishing. Many pursue it to the gates of prison, insanity, or death. (GA, 1989a, p. 2)

UNMANAGEABILITY

Imagine that you are the manager of a large corporation. You are responsible for how everything runs. If you are not a good manager, then the business will fail. You must carefully plan everything and carry out those plans well. You must be alert. You must know exactly where you are and where you are going. These are the skills that you need to manage your life effectively.

Gamblers are not good managers. They keep losing control. Their plans fall through. They cannot devise and stick to things long enough to see a solution. They are lying to themselves, so they do not know who they are. They feel confused. Their feelings are being changed by gambling, so they cannot use their feelings to give them energy and direction for problem solving.

You do not have to be a bad manager all of the time. It is worse to be a bad manager some of the time. It is very confusing. Most gamblers have flurries of productive activity during which they work too much. They work themselves to the bone, and then they let things slide. It is like being on a roller coaster. Sometimes things are in control, and sometimes things are out of control. Things are up and down, and gamblers never can predict which way things are going to be tomorrow.

People's lives are unmanageable when they have plans fall apart because they are gambling. Make a list of five plans that you failed to complete because of your gambling.

1. _____

2. _____

3. _____

4. _____

5. _____

People's lives are unmanageable when they cannot manage their finances consistently.

1. List the money problems that you are having.

_____

_____

_____

_____

_____

2. Explain how gambling has contributed to these problems.

_____

_____

_____

_____

_____

People's lives are unmanageable when they cannot trust their own judgments.

1. Have you ever been so absorbed in your gambling that you did not know what was happening around you? Explain.

_____

_____

_____

_____

_____

2. Did you ever lie to yourself about your gambling? Explain how your lies contributed to your being unable to manage your life.

_____

_____

_____

_____

_____

3. Have you ever made a decision while gambling that you were sorry about later? List five times.

1. _____

2. _____

3. _____

4. _____

5. _____

People's lives are unmanageable when they cannot work or play normally. Gamblers miss work and recreational activities because of their gambling.

List five times when you missed work because you were gambling.

1. _____

2. _____

3. _____

4. _____

5. _____

List five recreational or family activities because you were gambling.

1. _____

2. _____

3. _____

4. _____

5. _____

People's lives are unmanageable when they are in trouble with other people or society. Gamblers break the rules of society to get their own way. They have problems with authority.

1. Have you ever been in legal trouble when you were gambling? Explain the legal problems you have had.

_____

_____

_____

_____

_____

_____

2. Have you ever had problems with your parents because of your gambling? Explain.

_____

_____

_____

_____

_____

3. Have you ever had problems in school because of your gambling? Explain.

_____

_____

_____

_____

_____

People's lives are unmanageable when they cannot consistently achieve goals. Gamblers reach out for what they want, but something keeps getting in the way. It does not seem fair. They keep falling short of their goals. Finally, they give up completely. They may have had the goals of going to school, getting a better job, working on family problems, getting in good physical condition, and/or going on a diet. No matter what the goals are, something keeps going wrong with the plans. Gamblers constantly try to blame someone else, but they cannot work long enough to reach their goals. Gamblers are good starters, but they are poor finishers.

List five goals that you had for yourself that you did not achieve because of gambling.

1. _____

2. _____

3. _____

4. _____

5. _____

People's lives are unmanageable when they cannot use their feelings appropriately. Feelings give us energy and direction for problem solving. Gamblers change their feelings by staying in action. Gambling gives them a different feeling. Gamblers become very confused about how they feel.

1. What feelings have you tried to alter with gambling?

_____

_____

_____

_____

_____

2. How do you feel when you are gambling? Describe in detail.

_____

_____

_____

_____

_____

People's lives are unmanageable when they violate their own rules by violating their own morals and values. Gamblers compromise their values to continue gambling. They have the value not to lie, but they lie anyway. They have the value not to steal, but they steal anyway. They have the value to be loyal to spouses or friends, but when they are gambling they do not remain loyal. Their values and morals fall away, one by one. They end up doing things that they do not believe in. They know that they are doing the wrong things, but they do them anyway.

1. Did you ever lie to cover up your gambling? How did you feel about yourself?

_____

_____

_____

_____

_____

2. Were you ever disloyal when gambling? Explain.

_____

_____

_____

_____

_____

3. Did you ever steal or write bad checks to gamble? Explain what you did and how you felt about yourself later.

_____

_____

_____

_____

_____

4. Did you ever break the law when gambling? What did you do?

_____

_____

_____

_____

5. Did you ever hurt someone you loved while gambling? Explain.

_____

_____

_____

_____

6. Did you treat yourself poorly by refusing to stop gambling when you knew that it was bad for you? Explain how you were feeling about yourself.

_____

_____

_____

_____

7. Did you stop going to church? How did this make you feel about yourself?

_____

_____

_____

_____

People's lives are unmanageable when they continue to do something that gives them problems. Gambling creates severe financial problems. Even if gamblers are aware of the problems, they gamble anyway. They see gambling as the solution.

Gambling causes psychological problems. Compulsive gambling makes people feel depressed, fearful, anxious, and/or angry. Even when gamblers are aware of these symptoms, they continue to gamble.

Gambling creates relationship problems. It causes family problems in the form of family fights as well as verbal and physical abuse. It causes interpersonal conflict at work, with family, and with friends. Gamblers withdraw and become isolated and alone.

1. Did you have any persistent physical problems caused by or made worse by gambling? Describe the problems.

_____

_____

_____

_____

2. Did you have any persistent psychological problems, such as depression, that were caused by your gambling? Describe the problems.

_____

_____

_____

_____

3. Did you have persistent interpersonal conflicts that were made worse by gambling? Describe the problems.

_____

_____

_____

_____

_____

We know that no real compulsive gambler ever regains control. All of us felt at times we were regaining control, but such intervals—usually brief—were inevitably followed by still less control, which led in time to pitiful and incomprehensible demoralization. We are convinced that gamblers of our type are in the grip of a progressive illness. Over any considerable period of time, we get worse, never better. (GA, 1989a, p. 3)

You must have good reasons to work toward a new life free from gambling. Look over this exercise, and list 10 reasons why you want to stop gambling.

1. _____

2. _____

3. _____

4. _____

5. _____

6. _____

7. _____

8. _____

9. _____

10. _____

After completing this exercise, take a long look at yourself. What is the truth?

_____

_____

_____

1. Have there been times when you were powerless over gambling?

   Yes   No

2. Have there been times when your life was unmanageable?

   Yes   No

I am in the _____.

_____ Precontemplation stage

_____ Contemplation stage

_____ Preparation stage

_____ Action stage

_____ Maintenance stage

Step Two for Gamblers

[We] came to believe that a power greater than ourselves could restore us to a normal way of thinking and living.

—Gamblers Anonymous (GA) (1989b, p. 39)

Before beginning this exercise, please read Step Two in *G.A.: A New Beginning* (GA, 1989b).

In Step One, you admitted that you were powerless over gambling and that your life was unmanageable. In Step Two, you need to see the insanity of your disease and seek a power greater than yourself. If you are powerless, then you need power. If your life is unmanageable, then you need a manager. Step Two will help you to decide who that manager can be.

Most gamblers revolt at the implications of the phrase "restore to a normal way of thinking and living." They think that they may have a gambling problem, but they do not feel as though they have been abnormal.

In GA, the word *normal* means being of sound mind. Someone with a sound mind knows what is real and knows how to adapt to reality. A sound mind feels stable, safe, and secure. Someone who is abnormal cannot see reality and is unable to adapt. A person does not have to have all of reality distorted to be in trouble. If you miss some reality, then you ultimately will get lost. One wrong turn is all that it takes to end up in a ditch.

Going through life is like a long journey. You have a map given to you by your parents. The map shows the way in which to be happy. If you make some wrong turns along the way, then you will end up unhappy. This is what happens in gambling. In searching for happiness, we make wrong turns. We find out that our map is defective. Even if we followed our map to perfection, we still would be lost. What we need is a new map.

GA gives us this new map. It puts up 12 signposts to show us the way. If you follow this map—as millions of people have—then you will find the joy and happiness that you have been seeking. You have reached and passed the first signpost, Step One. You have decided that your life is powerless and unmanageable over gambling. Now you need a new power source. You need to find someone else who can manage your life.

GA is a spiritual program, and it directs you toward a spiritual solution. It is not a religious program. Spirituality is defined as the relationship you have with yourself and all else. Religion is an organized system of faith and worship. Everyone has spirituality, but not everyone has religion.

You need to explore three relationships very carefully in Step Two: (1) the relationships with yourself, (2) with others, and (3) with a Higher Power. This Higher Power can be any Higher Power of your choice. If you do not have a Higher Power right now, do not worry. Most of us started that way. Just be willing to consider that there is a power greater than you in the universe.

To explore these three relationships, you need to see the truth about yourself. If you see the truth, then you can find the way. First you must decide whether you were abnormal. Did you have a sound mind or not? Let us look at this issue carefully.

People are abnormal when they cannot remember what they did. They have memory problems. To be abnormal, they do not have to have memory problems all of the time; they just need to have them some of the time. People who gamble might not remember what happened to them when they were gambling. Long periods of time can pass during which gamblers are relatively unaware of their environment.

List any memory problems that you have had while gambling. Did you ever find that you had spent more time gambling than you remembered?

_____

_____

_____

_____

_____

People who are abnormal lose control over their behavior. They do things when they are gambling that they never would do otherwise.

List three times when you lost control over your behavior while gambling.

1. _____

2. _____

3. _____

List three times when you could not control your gambling—when you told yourself to stop but you could not.

1. _____

2. _____

3. _____

People who are abnormal consider self-destruction.

Did you ever consider hurting yourself when you were gambling or suffering from gambling losses?

Yes   No

Describe what happened.

_____

_____

_____

_____

People who are abnormal feel emotionally unstable.
Have you ever thought that you were going crazy because of your gambling?

Yes   No

Describe some of these times.

_____

_____

_____

_____

Have you recently felt emotionally unstable?

Yes   No

Describe how you have been feeling.

_____

_____

_____

_____

_____

People who are abnormal are so confused that they cannot get their lives in order. They frantically try to fix things, but problems remain out of control.

List 10 personal, family, work, or school problems that you have not been able to control.

1. _____

2. _____

3. _____

4. _____

5. _____

6. _____

7. _____

8. _____

9. _____

10. _____

People who are abnormal cannot see the truth about what is happening to them. People who are gambling hide their gambling from themselves and from others. They minimize, rationalize, and deny that there are problems.

Do you feel that you have been completely honest with yourself?

Yes   No

List five lies that you told yourself so you could continue gambling.

1. _____

2. _____

3. _____

4. _____

5. _____

People who are abnormal cut themselves off from healthy relationships. You might find that you cannot communicate with your spouse as well as you used to. You might not see your friends as often. More and more of your life centers around gambling.

List three people you do not see anymore because of your gambling.

1. _____

2. _____

3. _____

As your gambling increased, did you go to church less often?

Yes   No

List five relationships that you have damaged in your gambling.

1. _____

2. _____

3. _____

4. _____

5. _____

People who are abnormal cannot deal with their feelings. Problem gamblers cannot deal with their feelings. They do not like how they feel, so they gamble to control their feelings. Some people gamble to feel excited and some people gamble to escape.

List the feelings that you wanted to change by gambling.

_____

_____

_____

_____

_____

Now look back over your responses. Get out your Step One exercise and read it. Look at the truth about yourself. Look carefully at how you were thinking, feeling, and behaving when you were gambling. Make a decision. Do you think that you had a sound mind? If you were unsound at least some of the time, then you were abnormal. If you believe this to be true, then say this to yourself: "I am powerless. My life is unmanageable. My mind is unsound. I have been abnormal in thinking and living."

A POWER GREATER THAN OURSELVES

Consider a power greater than yourself. What exists in the world that has greater power than you do—a river, the wind, the universe, the sun?
List five things that have greater power than you do.

1. _____

2. _____

3. _____

4. _____

5. _____

The first Higher Power that you need to consider is the power of the GA group. The group is more powerful than you are. Ten hands are more powerful than two are. Two heads are better than one. GA operates in groups. The group works like a family. The group process is founded in love and trust. Each member shares his or her experiences, strengths, and hopes in an attempt to help him or her and others. There is an atmosphere of anonymity. What you hear in group is confidential.

The group acts as a mirror reflecting you to yourself. The group members will help you to discover the truth about whom and what you are. You have been deceiving yourself for a long time. The group will help you to uncover the lies. You will come to understand the old GA saying, "What we cannot do alone, we can do together." In group, you will have greater power over the disease because the group will see the whole truth better than you can.

You were not lying to hurt yourself; you were lying to protect yourself. In the process of building your lies, you cut yourself off from reality. This is how compulsive gambling works. You cannot recover from addiction by yourself. You need power coming from somewhere else. Begin by trusting your group. Keep an open mind.

You need to share in your group. The more you share, the closer you will get and the more trust you will develop. If you take risks, then you will reap the rewards. You do not have to tell the group everything, but you need to share as much as you can. The group can help you to straighten out your thinking and restore you to sanity.

Many gamblers are afraid of a Higher Power. They fear that a Higher Power will punish them or treat them in the same way that their fathers or mothers did. They might fear losing control. List some of the fears that you have about a Higher Power.

_____

_____

_____

_____

_____

Some gamblers have difficulty in trusting anyone. They have been so hurt by others that they do not want to take the chance of being hurt again. What has happened in your life that makes it difficult for you to trust?

_____

_____

_____

_____

What are some of the things you will need to see from a Higher Power that will show you that the Higher Power can be trusted?

_____

_____

_____

_____

_____

Who was the most trustworthy person you ever knew?

Name: _____

How did this person treat you?

_____

_____

_____

_____

What do you hope to gain by accepting a Higher Power?

_____

_____

_____

_____

GA wants you to come to believe in a power greater than yourself. You can accept any Higher Power that you feel can restore you to sanity. Your group, nature, your counselor, and your sponsor all can be used to give you this restoration. You must pick this Higher Power carefully. We suggest that you use GA as your Higher Power for now. Here is a group of people who are recovering. They have found the way. This program ultimately will direct you toward a God of your own understanding.

Millions of gamblers have recovered because they were willing to reach out for God. GA makes it clear that nothing else will remove the obsession to gamble. Some of us have so glorified our own lives that we have shut out God. Now is your opportunity. You are at a major turning point. You can begin to open your heart and let God in or you can keep God out. God tells us that all who seek will find.

Remember that this is the beginning of a new life. To be new, you have to do things differently. All that the program is asking you to do is be open to the possibility that there is a power greater than you are. GA does not demand that you believe in anything. The 12 steps are simply suggestions. You do not have to swallow all of this now, but you need to be open. Most recovering persons take the Second Step a piece at a time.

First you need to learn how to trust yourself. You must learn how to treat yourself well. What do you need to see from yourself that will show you that you are trustworthy?

_____

_____

_____

_____

_____

Then you need to begin to trust your group. See whether the group members act consistently in your interest. They will not always tell you what you want to hear. No real friend would do that. They will give you the opportunity and encouragement to grow. What will you need to see from the group members that will show you that they are trustworthy?

_____

_____

_____

_____

_____

Every person has a unique spiritual journey. No one can start this journey with a closed mind. What is it going to take to show you that God exists?

_____

_____

_____

_____

_____

Step Two does not mean that we believe in God as God is presented in any religion. Remember that religion is an organized system of worship. It is human-made. Worship is a means of assigning worth to something. Many people have been so turned off by religion that the idea of God is unacceptable. "We found that some of the obstacles preventing us from attempting to believe were pride, ego, fear, self-centeredness, defiance, and grandiosity" (GA, 1989b, p. 40).

Describe the religious environment of your childhood. What was it like? What did you learn about God?

_____

_____

_____

_____

How did these early experiences influence the beliefs that you have today?

_____

_____

_____

_____

What experiences have caused you to doubt God?

_____

_____

_____

_____

_____

Your willingness is essential to your recovery. Give some examples of your willingness to trust in a Higher Power of your choice. What are you willing to do?

_____

_____

_____

_____

Describe your current religious beliefs.

_____

_____

_____

_____

Explain the God of your own understanding.

_____

_____

_____

_____

List five reasons why a Higher Power will be good for you.

1. _____

2. _____

3. _____

4. _____

5. _____

If you asked the people in your GA group to describe God, you would get a variety of answers. Each person has his or her own understanding of God. It is this unique understanding that allows God to work individually for each of us. God comes to each of us differently.

I am in the _____.

_____ Precontemplation stage

_____ Contemplation stage

_____ Preparation stage

_____ Action stage

_____ Maintenance stage

Step Three for Gamblers

[We] made a decision to turn our will and our lives over to the care of this power of our own understanding.

—Gamblers Anonymous (GA) (1989b, p. 40)

Before beginning this exercise, please read Step Three in *G.A.: A New Beginning* (GA, 1989b).

You have come a long way in the program, and you can feel proud of yourself. You have decided that you are powerless over gambling and that your life is unmanageable. You have decided that a Higher Power of some sort can restore you to normal thinking and living.

In Step Three, you will reach toward a Higher Power of your own understanding. This is the miracle. It is the major focus of the GA program. This is a spiritual program that directs you toward the ultimate in truth. It is important that you be open to the possibility that there is a God. It is vital that you give this concept room to blossom and grow.

Many of us used our sponsor, other members, or the fellowship as this Higher Power, but eventually, as we proceeded with the work required in these steps, we came to believe this Higher Power to be a God of our own understanding. (GA, 1989b, p. 40)

Step Three should not confuse you. It calls for a decision to correct your character defects under spiritual supervision. You must make an honest effort to change your life.

The GA program is a spiritual one. Gamblers in recovery must have the honesty to look at their illness, the open-mindedness to apply the solution being told to themselves, and the willingness to apply this solution by proceeding on with the recovery process. If you are willing to seek God, then you will find God. That is the GA promise.

THE MORAL LAW

All spirituality has, at its core, what is already inside of you. Your Higher Power lives inside of you. Inside of all of us, there is inherent goodness. In all cultures, and in all lands, this goodness is expressed in what we call the moral law. Morality demands love in action and in truth. It is simply stated as follows: Love God all you can, love others all you can, and love yourself all you can. This law is very powerful. If some stranger were drowning in a pool next to you, then this law would motivate you to help. Instinctively, you would feel driven to help, even if it put your own life at risk. The moral law is so important that it transcends our instinct for survival. You would try to save that drowning person at your own risk. This moral law is exactly the same everywhere—in every culture. It exists inside of everyone. It is written on our hearts. Even among thieves, honesty is valued.

When we survey religious thought, we come up with many different ideas about God and about how to worship God. When we look at saints of the various religions, we see that they are living practically indistinguishable lives. They all are doing the same things. They do not lie, cheat, or steal. They believe in giving to others before they give to themselves. They try not to be envious of others. To believe in a Higher Power, you must believe that this good exists inside of you. You also must believe that there is more of this good outside of you. If you do not believe in a living, breathing God at this point, do not worry. Every one of us has started where you are.

All people have a basic problem: We break the moral law, even if we believe in it. This fact means that something is wrong with us. We are incapable of following the moral law. Even though we would deem it unfair for someone to lie to us, occasionally we lie to someone else. If we see someone dressed in clothes that look terrible, then we might tell the person that he or she looks good. This is a lie. We would not want other people lying to us like that. In this and other situations, we do not obey the very moral law that we know is good.

You must ask yourself several questions. Where did we get this moral law? How did this law of behavior get started? Did it just evolve? The GA program believes that these good laws come from something good. People in the program believe that you can communicate with this goodness.

Much of God remains a mystery. If we look at science, we find the same thing; most of science is a mystery. We know very little about the primary elements of science such as gravity, but we make judgments about these elements using our experience. No one has ever seen an electron, but we are sure that it exists because we have some experience of it. It is the same with the Higher Power. We can know that there is a power greater than we are if we have some experience of this power. Both science and spirituality necessitate a faith based on experience.

Instinctively, people know that if they can get more goodness that they will have better lives. Spirituality must be practical. It must make your life better or you will discard it. If you open yourself up to the spiritual part of the program, then you will feel better immediately.

By reading this exercise, you can begin to develop your relationship with a Higher Power. You will find true joy here if you try. Without some sort of a Higher Power, your recovery will be more difficult. A Higher Power can relieve your gambling problem as nothing else can. Many people achieve stable recovery without calling their Higher Power "God." That certainly is possible. There are many wonderful atheists and agnostics in our program. The GA way is to reach for a God of your own understanding.

You can change things in your life. You really can. You do not have to drown in despair any longer.

THE KEY TO STEP THREE

The key to working Step Three is willingness. You must have the willingness to turn your life over to the care of God as you understand God. This is difficult for many of us because we think that we are still in control. We are completely fooled by this delusion. We feel as though we know the right thing to do. We feel that everything would be fine if others would just do things our way. This leads us to deep feelings of resentment and self-pity. People would not cooperate with our plan. No matter how hard we tried to control everything, things kept getting out of control. Sometimes the harder we worked, the worse things got.

HOW TO TURN IT OVER

To arrest gambling, you have to stop playing God and let the God of your own understanding take control. If you sincerely want this and you try, then it is easy. Go to a quiet place and talk to your Higher Power about your gambling. Say something like this: "God, I am lost. I cannot do this anymore. I turn this situation over to you." Watch how you feel when you say this prayer. The next time you have a problem, stop and turn the problem over to your Higher Power. Say something like this: "God, I cannot deal with this problem. You deal with it." See what happens.

Your Higher Power wants to show you the way. If you try to find the way yourself, you will be constantly lost.

Step Three offers no compromise. It calls for a decision. Exactly how we surrender and turn things over is not the point. The important thing is that you be willing to try. Can you see that it is necessary to give up your self-centeredness? Do you feel that it is time to turn things over to a power greater than you are?

List five things you have to gain by turning your will and your life over to a Higher Power.

1. _____

2. _____

3. _____

4. _____

5. _____

Why do you need to turn things over to a Higher Power?

_____

_____

_____

_____

_____

We should not confuse organized religion with spirituality. In Step Two, you learned that spirituality deals with your relationships with yourself, with others, and with your Higher Power. Religion is an organized system of faith and worship. It is human-made, not God-made. It is humans' way of interpreting God. Religion can be very confusing, and it can drive people away from God. Are old religious ideas keeping you from God? If so, then how?

_____

_____

_____

_____

A great barrier to finding your Higher Power may be impatience. You may want to find God right now. You must understand that your spiritual growth is not set by you. You will grow spiritually when God feels that you are ready. Remember that we are turning this whole thing over. Each person has his or her unique spiritual journey. Each individual must have his or her own walk. Spiritual growth, not perfection, is your goal. All that you can do is seek the God of your understanding. When God knows that you are ready, God will find you.

Total surrender is necessary. If you are holding back, then you need to let go absolutely. Faith, willingness, and prayer will overcome all of the obstacles. Do not worry about your doubt. Just keep seeking.

List 10 ways in which you can seek God. Ask someone in the program, a clergyperson, or your counselor to help you.

1. _____

2. _____

3. _____

4. _____

5. _____

6. _____

7. _____

8. _____

9. _____

10. _____

What does the saying "Let go and let God" mean to you?

_____

_____

_____

_____

_____

_____

_____

What are five ways in which you can put Step Three to work in your life?

1. _____

2. _____

3. _____

4. _____

5. _____

What things in your life do you still want to control?

_____

_____

_____

_____

How can these things be handled better by turning them over to your Higher Power?

_____

_____

_____

_____

List five ways in which you allowed gambling to be the God in your life.

1. _____

2. _____

3. _____

4. _____

5. _____

How did gambling separate you from God?

_____

_____

_____

_____

_____

What changes have you noticed in yourself since you entered the program?

_____

_____

_____

_____

_____

Of these changes, which of them occurred because you listened to someone other than yourself?

_____

_____

_____

_____

Make a list of five things that are holding you back from turning things over to God.

1. _____

2. _____

3. _____

4. _____

5. _____

How do you see God caring for you?

_____

_____

_____

_____

_____

How do you understand God now?

_____

_____

_____

_____

_____

Write down your spiritual plan. What are five things are you going to do on a daily basis to help your spiritual program grow?

1. _____

2. _____

3. _____

4. _____

5. _____

I am in the _____.

_____ Precontemplation stage

_____ Contemplation stage

_____ Preparation stage

_____ Action stage

_____ Maintenance stage

Step Four for Gamblers

> [We] made a searching and fearless moral and financial inventory of ourselves.
>
> —Gamblers Anonymous (GA) (1989b, p. 68)

Before beginning this exercise, please read Step Four in *G.A.: A New Beginning* (GA, 1989b).

You are doing well in the program. You have admitted your powerlessness over gambling, and you have found a Higher Power that can restore you to normal thinking and living. Now you must take an inventory of yourself. You must know exactly what resources you have available, and you must examine the exact nature of your wrongs. You need to be detailed about the good things about you as well as the bad things about you. Only by taking this inventory will you know exactly where you are. Then you can decide where you are going.

In taking this inventory, you must be detailed and specific. It is the only way of seeing the complete impact of your disease. A part of the truth might be the following: "I told lies to my children." The complete truth might be, "I told my children that I had cancer. They were terrified and cried for a long time." These two statements would be very different. Only the second statement tells the exact nature of the wrong, and the client felt the full impact of the disclosure. You can see how important it is to put the whole truth before you at one time—the truth that will set you free.

The Fourth Step is a long autobiography. You can write it down carefully. Read this exercise before you start, and underline things that pertain to you. You will want to come back and cover each of these issues in detail as you write it down. If the problem does not relate to you, then leave it blank. Examine exactly what you did wrong. Look for your mistakes—even where the situations were not totally your fault. Try to disregard what the other person did, and concentrate on yourself instead. In time, you will realize that the person who hurt you was spiritually sick. You need to ask God to help you forgive that person and to show that person the same understanding that you would want for yourself. You can pray that this person finds out the truth about himself or herself.

Review your natural desires carefully, and think about how you acted on them. You will see that some of them became the God of your life. Sex, food, money, relationships, sleep, power, and influence all can become the major focus of our lives. The pursuit of these desires can take total control and can become the center of our existence.

Review your sexuality as you move through the inventory. Did you ever use someone else selfishly? Did you ever lie to get what you wanted? Did you coerce or force someone into doing something that he or she did not want to do? Whom did you hurt, and exactly what did you do?

In working through the inventory, you will experience some pain. You will feel angry, sad, afraid, ashamed, embarrassed, guilty, and lonely. The Fourth Step is a grieving process. As you see your wrongs clearly, you may feel that no one will ever love you again. Remember that God created you in perfection. You are God's masterpiece. There is nothing wrong with you. You just made some mistakes.

Now let us take a basic look at right and wrong.

1. *Pride:* Too great an admiration of yourself

Pride makes you your own law, your own moral judge, and your own God. Pride produces criticism, backstabbing, slander, barbed words, and character assassinations that elevate your own ego. Pride makes you condemn as fools those who criticize you. Pride gives you excuses. It produces the following:

a. Boasting or self-glorification

b. Love of publicity

c. Hypocrisy or pretending to be better than you are

d. Hardheadedness or refusing to give up your will

e. Discord or resenting anyone who crosses you

f. Quarrelsomeness or quarreling whenever another person challenges your wishes

g. Disobedience or refusing to submit your will to the will of superiors or to God

2. *Covetousness or avarice:* Perversion of humans' God-given right to own things

Do you desire wealth in the form of money or other things as an end in itself rather than as a means to an end such as taking care of the soul and body? In acquiring wealth in any form, do you disregard the rights of others? Are you dishonest? If so, then to what degree and in what fashion? Do you give an honest day's work for an honest day's pay? How do you use what you have? Are you stingy with your family? Do you love money and possessions for these things in themselves? How excessive is your love of luxury? How do you preserve your wealth or increase it? Do you stoop to devices such as fraud, perjury, dishonesty, and sharp practices in dealing with others? Do you try to fool yourself in these regards? Do you call stinginess "thrift"? Do you call questionable business "big business" or "drive"? Do you call unreasonable hoarding "security"? If you currently have no money and little other wealth, then how and by what practice will you go about getting it later? Will you do almost anything to attain these things and kid yourself by giving your methods innocent names?

3. *Lust:* Inordinate love and desires of the pleasures of the flesh

Are you guilty of lust in any of its forms? Do you tell yourself that improper or undue indulgence in sexual activities is required? Do you treat people as objects of your desire rather than as God's perfect creations? Do you use pornography or think unhealthy sexual thoughts? Do you treat other people sexually the same way in which you want to be treated?

4. *Envy:* Sadness at another person's good

How envious are you? Do you dislike seeing others happy or successful, almost as though they have taken from you? Do you resent those who are smarter than you are? Do you ever criticize the good done by others because you secretly wish you had done it yourself for the honor or prestige to be gained? Are you ever envious enough to try to lower another person's reputation by starting, or engaging in, gossip about that person? Being envious includes calling religious people "hypocrites" because they go to church and try to be religiously good even though they are subject to human failings. Do you depreciate well-bred people by saying or feeling that they put on airs? Do you ever accuse educated, wise, or learned people of being conceited because you envy their advantages? Do you genuinely love other people, or do you find them distasteful because you envy them?

5. *Anger:* A violent desire to punish others

Do you ever fly into rages of temper, become revengeful, entertain urges to "get even," or express an "I will not let him get away with it" attitude? Do you ever resort to violence, clench your fists, or stomp about in a temper flare-up? Are you touchy, unduly sensitive, or impatient at the smallest slight? Do you ever murmur or grumble, even regarding small matters? Do you ignore the fact that anger prevents development of personality and halts spiritual progress? Do you realize at all times that anger disrupts mental poise and often ruins good judgment? Do you permit anger to rule you when you know that it blinds you to the rights of others? How can you excuse even small tantrums of temper when anger destroys the spirit of recollection that you need for compliance with the inspirations of God? Do you permit yourself to become angry when others are weak and become angry with you? Can you hope to entertain the serene spirit of God within your soul when you often are beset by angry flare-ups of even minor importance?

6. *Gluttony:* Abuse of lawful pleasures that God attached to eating and drinking of foods required for self-preservation

Do you weaken your moral and intellectual life by excessive use of food and drink? Do you generally eat to excess and, thus, enslave your soul and character to the pleasures of the body beyond its reasonable needs? Do you kid yourself that you can be a "hog" without affecting your moral life? When gambling, did you ever win big, only to return and immediately gamble to win more? Did you gamble so much that your intellect and personality deteriorated? So much that memory, judgment, and concentration were affected? So much that personal pride and social judgment vanished? So much that you developed a spirit of despair?

7. *Sloth:* Laziness of the will that causes a neglect of duty

Are you lazy or given to idleness, procrastination, nonchalance, and indifference in material things? Are you lukewarm in prayer? Do you hold self-discipline in contempt? Would you rather read a novel than study something requiring brain work such as the GA (1989b) book? Are you fainthearted in performance of those things that are morally or spiritually difficult? Are you ever listless with aversion to effort in any form? Are you easily distracted from things spiritual, quickly turning to things temporal? Are you ever indolent to the extent where you perform work carelessly?

PERSONALITY DEFECTS

1. *Selfishness:* Taking care of your own needs without regard for others
   a. The family would like to go on an outing. Dad would like gambling, golfing, and fishing. Who wins?
   b. Your child needs a new pair of shoes. You put it off until payday but then gamble away the paycheck.
   c. You are afraid to dance because you might appear awkward. You fear any new venture because it might injure the false front that you put on.

2. *Alibis:* The highly developed art of justifying gambling and behavior through mental gymnastics
   a. "A few dollars will not hurt anything."
   b. "Starting tomorrow, I am going to change."
   c. "If I did not have a wife and family…"
   d. "If I could start all over again…"
   e. "A little gambling will help me to relax."
   f. "Nobody cares anyway."
   g. "I had a hard day."

3. *Dishonest thinking:* Another way of lying

   We may even take truths or facts and, through some phony hopscotch, come up with exactly the conclusions that we had planned to arrive at. Boy, we are great at that business.
   a. "My secret love is going to raise the roof if I drop her. It is not fair to burden my wife with that sort of knowledge. Therefore, I will hang on to my girlfriend. This mess isn't her fault." (good solid con)
   b. "If I tell my family about the $500 bonus, then it will all go for bills, clothes, the dentist, and so on. I have to have some gambling money. Why start a family argument? I would leave well enough alone."
   c. "My husband dresses well, he eats well, and the kids are getting a good education. What more do they want from me?"

4. *Shame:* The feeling that something irreparable is wrong with you
   a. No matter how many people tell you it is okay, you continue to berate yourself.
   b. You keep going over and over your mistakes, wallowing in what a terrible person you are.

5. *Resentment:* Displeasure aroused by a real or imagined wrong or injury accompanied by irritation, exasperation, and/or hate
   a. You are fired from your job. Therefore, you hate the boss.
   b. Your sister warns you about excessive gambling. You get fighting mad at her.
   c. A coworker is doing a good job and gets accolades. You have a legal record and suspect that he might have been promoted over you. You hate his guts.

d. You may have resentment toward a person or a group of people or you may resent institutions, religions, and so on. Anger and resentment lead to bickering, friction, hatred, and unjust revenge. They bring out the worst of our immaturity and produce misery to ourselves.

6. *Intolerance:* Refusal to put up with beliefs, practices, customs, or habits that differ from our own

   a. Do you hate other people because they are of another race, come from a different country, or have a different religion? What would you do if you were one of those other persons? Kill yourself?

   b. Did you have any choice in being born a particular color or nationality?

   c. Isn't our religion usually "inherited"?

7. *Impatience:* Unwillingness to bear delay, opposition, pain, or bother

   a. A pathological gambler is someone who jumps on a horse and gallops off madly in all directions at the same time.

   b. Do you blow your stack when someone keeps you waiting over the "allotted time" that you gave that person?

   c. Did anyone ever have to wait for you?

8. *Phoniness:* A manifestation of our great false pride; a form of lying; rank and brash dishonesty; the old false front

   a. "I give to my love a present as evidence of my love. Just by pure coincidence, it helps to smooth over my last binge."

   b. "I buy new clothes because my business position demands it. Meanwhile, the family also could use food and clothes."

   c. A joker may enthrall a GA audience with profound wisdom but not give the time of day to his or her spouse or children.

9. *Procrastination:* Putting off or postponing things that need to be done; the familiar "I will do it tomorrow"

   a. Did little jobs, when put off, become big and almost impossible later? Did problems piling up contribute to gambling?

   b. Do you pamper yourself by doing things "my way," or do you attempt to put order and discipline into your life?

   c. Can you handle little jobs that you are asked to take care of, or do you feel picked on? Are you just too lazy or proud?

10. *Self-pity:* An insidious personality defect and a danger signal to look for

    Stop self-pity in a hurry. It is the buildup to trouble.

    a. "These people at the party are having fun with their gambling. Why can't I be like that?" This is the "woe is me" syndrome.

    b. "If I had that guy's money, I would not have any problems." When you feel this way, visit a cancer ward or children's hospital and then count your blessings.

11. *Feelings easily hurt:* Overly sensitive to the slightest criticism
    a. "I walk down the street and say 'Hello' to someone. They do not answer. I am hurt and mad."
    b. "I am expecting my turn at the GA meeting, but the time runs out. I feel as though that is a dirty trick."
    c. "I feel as though they are talking about me at meetings when they're really not."

12. *Fear:* An inner foreboding, real or imagined, of doom ahead

    We suspect that our use of gambling, behavior, negligence, and so on is catching up with us. We fear the worst.

    When we learn to accept our powerlessness, ask God for help, and face ourselves with honesty, the nightmare will be over.

13. *Depression:* Feeling sad or down most of the day
    a. You keep going over all of the things that are going wrong.
    b. You tend to think that the worst is going to happen.

14. *Feelings of inadequacy:* Feeling as though you cannot do something
    a. You hold on to a negative self-image, even when you succeed.
    b. Feelings of failure will not go away.

15. *Perfectionism:* The need to do everything perfect all of the time
    a. Even when you have done a good job, you find something wrong with it.
    b. Someone compliments you on something. You feel terrible because it could have been better.
    c. You let your expectations get too high.

PHYSICAL LIABILITIES

1. Diseases, disabilities, and other physical limitations about how you look or how your body functions

2. Sexual problems or hang-ups

3. Negative feelings about your appearance

4. Negative feelings about your age

5. Negative feelings about your gender

TIME-OUT

If you have gone through the exercise to this point without coming up for air—it figures. We did our gambling the same way. Whoa! Easy does it! Take this in reasonable stages. Assimilate each portion of the exercise thoughtfully. The reading of this is important, but the application of it is even more important. Take some time to think and rest, and let this settle in. Develop some sort of a workable daily plan. Include plenty of rest.

When compulsive gamblers stop gambling, a part of their lives are taken away from them. This is a terrible loss to sustain unless it is replaced by something else. We cannot just boot gambling out the window. It meant too much to us. It was how we faced life, the key to escape, and the tool for solving life's problems. In approaching a new way of life, a new set of tools is substituted. These are the 12 steps and the GA way of life.

The same principle applies when we eliminate our character defects. We replace them by substituting assets that are better adapted to a healthy lifestyle. As with substance use, you do not fight a defect; you replace it with something that works better. Use what follows for further character analysis and as a guide for character building. These are the new tools. The objective is not perfection; it is progress. You will be happy with the type of living that produces self-respect, respect and love for others, and security from the nightmare of gambling.

THE WAY TO RECOVERY

1. *Faith:* The act of leaving the part of our lives that we cannot control (i.e., the future) to the care of a power greater than ourselves, with the assurance that it will work out for our well-being.

   This will be shaky at first, but with it comes a deep conviction.

   a. Faith is acquired through application—acceptance, daily prayer, and meditation.

   b. We depend on faith. We have faith that the lights will come on, the car will start, and our coworkers will handle their end of things. If we had no faith, then we would come apart at the seams.

   c. Spiritual faith is the acceptance of our gifts, limitations, problems, and trials with equal gratitude, knowing that God has a plan for us. With "Thy will be done" as our daily guide, we will lose our fear and find ourselves.

2. *Hope:* This is the feeling that what is desired also is possible.

   Faith suggests reliance. We came to believe that a power greater than ourselves would restore us to sanity. We hope to stay free of gambling, regain our self-respect, and love our families. Hope resolves itself into a driving force. It gives purpose to our daily living.

   a. Faith gives us direction, hope, and stamina to take action.

   b. Hope reflects a positive attitude. Things are going to work out for us if we work the program.

3. *Love:* This is active involvement in someone's individual growth.

   a. Love must occur in action and in truth.

   b. Love is patient, gentle, and kind.

   c. In its deeper sense, love is the art of living realistically and fully, guided by spiritual awareness of our responsibilities and our debt of gratitude to God and to others.

Analysis. Have you used the qualities of faith, hope, and love in your past? How will they apply to your new way of life?

_____

_____

_____

_____

_____

_____

WE STAY ON TRACK THROUGH ACTION

1. *Courtesy:* Some of us are actually afraid to be gentle persons. We would rather be boors or self-pampering types.

2. *Cheerfulness:* Circumstances do not determine our frames of mind. We do. "Today I will be cheerful. I will look for the beauty in life."

3. *Order:* Live today only. Organize one day at a time.

4. *Loyalty:* Be faithful to who you believe in.

5. *Use of time:* "I will use my time wisely."

6. *Punctuality:* This involves self-discipline, order, and consideration for others.

7. *Sincerity:* This is the mark of self-respect and genuineness. Sincerity carries conviction and generates enthusiasm. It is contagious.

8. *Caution in speech:* Watch your tongue. We can be vicious and thoughtless. Too often, the damage is irreparable.

9. *Kindness:* This is one of life's great satisfactions. We do not have real happiness until we have given of ourselves. Practice this daily.

10. *Patience:* This is the antidote to resentments, self-pity, and impulsiveness.

11. *Tolerance:* This requires common courtesy, courage, and a "live and let live" attitude.

12. *Integrity:* This involves the ultimate qualifications of a human—honesty, loyalty, sincerity.

13. *Balance:* Do not take yourself too seriously. You get a better perspective when you can laugh at yourself.

14. *Gratitude:* The person without gratitude is filled with false pride. Gratitude is the honest recognition of help received. Use it often.

Analysis. In considering the little virtues, ask where you failed and how that contributed to your accumulated problem. Ask what virtues you should pay attention to in this rebuilding program.

_____

_____

_____

_____

_____

PHYSICAL ASSETS

1. *Physical health:* How healthy am I despite any ailments?

_____

_____

_____

_____

_____

2. *Talents:* What do I do that is good?

_____

_____

_____

_____

_____

3. *Age:* At my age, what can I offer to others?

_____

_____

_____

_____

_____

4. *Sexuality:* How can I use my sexuality to express my love?

_____

_____

_____

_____

_____

5. *Knowledge:* How can I use my knowledge and experience to help others and myself?

_____

_____

_____

_____

_____

MENTAL ASSETS

1. Despite your problems, how healthy are you emotionally?

_____

_____

_____

_____

_____

2. Do you care for others?

_____

_____

_____

_____

_____

3. Are you kind?

_____

_____

_____

_____

_____

4. Can you be patient?

_____

_____

_____

_____

_____

5. Are you basically a good person?

_____

_____

_____

_____

_____

6. Do you try to tell the truth?

_____

_____

_____

_____

7. Do you try to be forgiving?

_____

_____

_____

_____

_____

8. Can you be enthusiastic?

_____

_____

_____

_____

9. Are you sensitive to the needs of others?

_____

_____

_____

_____

10. Can you be serene?

_____

_____

_____

_____

_____

11. Are you going to try to be sincere?

_____

_____

_____

_____

12. Are you going to try to bring order and self-control into your life?

_____

_____

_____

_____

13. Are you going to accept the responsibility for your own behavior and stop blaming others for everything?

_____

_____

_____

_____

14. How are you going to use your intelligence?

_____

_____

_____

_____

_____

15. Are you going to seek God?

_____

_____

_____

_____

_____

16. How might you improve your mind furthering your education?

_____

_____

_____

_____

_____

17. Are you going to be grateful for what you have?

_____

_____

_____

_____

_____

18. How can you improve your honesty, reliability, and integrity?

_____

_____

_____

_____

19. In what areas of your life do you find joy and happiness?

_____

_____

_____

_____

20. Are you humble and working on your false pride?

_____

_____

_____

_____

21. Are you seeking the God of your own understanding?

_____

_____

_____

_____

_____

22. In what ways can you better accept your own limitations and the limitations of others?

_____

_____

_____

_____

23. Are you willing to trust and follow the Higher Power of your own understanding?

_____

_____

_____

_____

THE AUTOBIOGRAPHY

Using this exercise, write your autobiography. Cover your life in 5-year intervals. Be brief, but try not to miss anything. Tell the whole truth. Write down exactly what you did. Consider all of the things you marked during the exercise. Read the exercise again if you need to do so. Make an exhaustive and honest consideration of your past and present. Make a complete financial inventory. Mark down all debts. Exactly who do you owe, and what amount do you owe? Do not leave out relatives or friends. List all persons or institutions that you harmed with your gambling, and detail exactly how you were unfair. Cover both assets and liabilities carefully. You will rebuild your life on the solid building blocks of your assets. These are the tools of recovery. Omit nothing because of shame, embarrassment, or fear. Determine the thoughts, feelings, and actions that plagued you. You want to meet these problems face to face and see them in writing. If you wish, you may destroy your inventory after completing the Fifth Step. Many people hold a ceremony in which they burn their Fourth Step inventories. This symbolizes that they are leaving the old life behind. They are starting a new life free of the past.

I am in the _____.

_____ Precontemplation stage

_____ Contemplation stage

_____ Preparation stage

_____ Action stage

_____ Maintenance stage

Step Five for Gamblers

[We] admitted to ourselves and to another human being the exact nature of our wrongs.

—Gamblers Anonymous (GA) (1989b, p. 69)

Before beginning this exercise, please read Step Five in *G.A.: A New Beginning* (GA, 1989b).

With Steps One through Four behind you, it is now time to clean house and start over. You must free yourself of all the guilt and shame and go forward in faith. The Fifth Step is meant to right the wrongs with others and the Higher Power. You will develop new attitudes and a new relationship with yourself, others, and the Higher Power of your own understanding. You have admitted your powerlessness, and you have identified your liabilities and assets in the personal inventory. Now it is time to get right with yourself.

You will do this by admitting to yourself—and to another person—the exact nature of your wrongs. In your Fifth Step, you are going to cover all of your assets and liabilities detailed in the Fourth Step. You are going to tell one person the whole truth at one time. This person is important because he or she is a symbol of the Higher Power and all humankind. You must watch this person's face. The illness has been telling you that if you tell anyone the whole truth about you then that person will not like you. That is a lie, and you are going to prove that it is a lie. The truth is this: Unless you tell people the whole truth, they cannot like you. You must actually see yourself tell someone the whole truth at one time and watch that individual's reaction.

It is very difficult to discuss your faults with someone. It is hard enough just thinking about them yourself. This is a necessary step. It will help to free you from the disease. You must tell this person everything—the whole story—all of the things that you are afraid to share. If you withhold anything, then you will not get the relief you need to start over. You will be carrying around excess baggage. You do not need to do this to yourself. Time after time, newcomers have tried to keep to themselves certain facts about their lives. Trying to avoid this humbling experience, they have turned to easier methods. Almost invariably, they wound up gambling again. Having persevered with the rest of the program, they wondered why they failed. The reason is that they never completed their housecleaning. They took inventory all right, but they hung on to some of the worst items in stock. They only *thought* that they had lost their egotism. They only *thought* that they had humbled themselves. They had not learned enough of humility and honesty in the sense necessary until they told someone their whole life stories.

By finally telling someone the whole truth, you will rid yourself of that terrible sense of isolation and loneliness. You will feel a new sense of belonging, acceptance, and freedom. If you do not feel relief immediately, do not worry. If you have been completely honest, then the relief will come. The dammed-up emotions of years will break out of their confinement and, miraculously, will vanish as soon as they are exposed.

The Fifth Step will develop within you a new humbleness of character that is necessary for normal living. You will come to recognize clearly who and what you are. When you are honest with another person, it confirms that you can be honest with yourself, others, and your Higher Power.

The person who you will share your Fifth Step with should be chosen carefully. Many of us find a clergyperson, experienced in hearing Fifth Steps, to be a good option. Someone further along in the GA program might also be a good choice. It is recommended that you meet with this person several times before you do the step. You need to decide whether you can trust this person. Do you feel that this person is confidential? Do you feel comfortable with this person? Do you feel that this person will understand?

Once you have chosen the person, put your false pride aside and go for it. Tell the individual everything about yourself. Do not leave one rock unturned. Tell about all of the good things and about all of the bad things you have done. Share the details, and do not leave anything out. If it troubles you even a little, then share it. Let it all hang out to be examined by that other person. Every good and bad part needs to be revealed. After you are done, you will be free of the slavery to lies. The truth will set you free.

I am in the _____.

_____ Precontemplation stage

_____ Contemplation stage

_____ Preparation stage

_____ Action stage

_____ Maintenance stage

Relapse Prevention for Gamblers

There is some bad news and some good news about relapse. The bad news is that many clients have problems with relapse in early recovery. About two thirds of clients coming out of addiction programs relapse within 3 months of leaving treatment (Hunt, Barnett, & Branch, 1971). The good news is that most people who go through treatment ultimately achieve a stable recovery (Frances, Bucky, & Alexopolos, 1984). Relapse does not have to happen to you, and even if it does, you can do something about it. Relapse prevention is a daily program that can help prevent relapse. It also can stop a lapse from becoming a disaster. This exercise has been developed using a combination of the models. This uses the disease concept model in combination with motivational enhancement, cognitive behavioral therapy, skills training, and 12-step facilitation.

RELAPSE IS A PROCESS

Relapse is a process that begins long before you gamble. There are symptoms that precede the first gambling episode. This exercise teaches you how to identify and control these symptoms before they lead to gambling. If you allow these symptoms to go on without acting on them, then serious problems will result.

THE RELAPSE WARNING SIGNS

All relapse begins with warning signs that will signal for you that you are in trouble. If you do not recognize these signs, you will decompensate and finally gamble. All of the signs are a reaction to stress, and they are a reemergence of the disease. They are a means by which your body and mind are telling you that you are in trouble. You might not have all of these symptoms, but you will have some of them long before you actually use chemicals. You must determine which symptoms are the most characteristic of you, and you must come up with coping skills for dealing with each symptom.

Interpersonal Factors

- Self-efficacy is the degree you feel capable of performing a task such as preventing relapse. Do you feel confident that you have the skills necessary to say no to the addiction when confronted with a high-risk situation including intense craving? Do you have the skills necessary to say no to gambling?

- Make a list of 10 things you can do when you feel the urge to gamble. There are people you can call, meetings you can attend, things you can read, a higher power you can pray to, family members, friends or people in the program you can share your feelings with, the Gamblers Anonymous (GA) hotline, someone you can call in the program, physical exercise you can do, meditations you can perform, etc.

1. _____

2. _____

3. _____

4. _____

5. _____

6. _____

7. _____

8. _____

9. _____

10. _____

Practice each of these 10 things at least five times in group, with your counselor/sponsor/mentor/coach. You need to get used to thinking and moving in a certain way when faced with craving. If these behaviors are not practiced in skills training sessions they are unlikely to be used when you get into trouble. Just knowing what to do is not enough; you need to practice the thoughts and motor movements to get good at the skill.

Think about the first time you learned how to ride a bike. Your teacher probably taught you all of the things you had to do to ride, but it was only after you practiced riding, repeatedly, that you began to trust yourself to ride a bike safely.

Make a list of five things in your life that you had to practice. Maybe it was basketball, baseball, soccer, or starting a conversation with someone you did not know.

1. _____

2. _____

3. _____

4. _____

5. _____

At first you were terrible, making mostly mistakes, but after practicing thousands of times you got better. Maybe you had to learn how to shoot a basket from the free throw line. The first times you tried, you missed almost every shot. As you practiced—and particularly after you were coached—you got better. After thousands of shots, you got so you could make the shot most of the time. Then there came the big game, and the score was tied and you had to shoot the final basket. If you made the shot, your team won; if you missed the shot, you lost. Now you need to practice so much that you go on automatic—athletes call this getting in the zone, where all of the fans and other players disappear and it is only you and that simple shot you have practiced so many times. If you miss the shot or lapse, it is not the end of the world; it just means you need more practice until the skill becomes automatic.

Higher levels of self-efficacy predict improved addiction treatment outcomes (Burling, Reilly, Molten, & Ziff, 1989; Greenfield et al., 2000).

WHEN YOU EXPERIENCE A WARNING SIGN

When you recognize you are in trouble, you need to take action. Make a list of the coping skills you can use when you experience a high-risk situation that is common for you. It might be interpersonal conflict, anger, boredom, certain music or parts of town, seeing old friends, social pressure, negative emotions, or a celebration. This will happen. You will have high-risk situations in recovery (Marlatt & Donovan, 2008; Marlatt & Gordon, 1985; Shaffer & LaPlante, 2008). Your task is to take affirmative action. Remember, craving is a danger signal. You are in trouble. Make a list of what you are going to do. Are you going to call your sponsor, go to a meeting, call your counselor, call someone in GA, tell someone, exercise, read the problem gambling material, pray, become involved in an activity you enjoy, turn it over, or go into treatment? List five telephone numbers of people you can call if you are in trouble. Remember what GA says, "What we cannot do alone, we can do together."

Plan 1.

_____

_____

_____

_____

_____

Plan 2.

_____

_____

_____

_____

Plan 3.

_____

_____

_____

_____

Plan 4.

_____

_____

_____

_____

Plan 5.

_____

_____

_____

_____

_____

Positive Outcome Expectations

This means the positive things we think will happen if we gamble. These are dangerous thoughts and if not corrected may lead to relapse. Write down five positive thoughts about what gambling can do for you. For example: "One bet will not hurt." "I deserve to relax." "I would only bet one time." "I have had a hard day." "I need to relax at the casino." "Nobody will know." "I am going to show them." "I am going to get even." "I am going to make them sorry." "I am under too much stress." "I need a break."

1. _____

2. _____

3. _____

4. _____

5. _____

Now write down 10 accurate thoughts that will keep you from gambling. For example: "I cannot make one bet because I am a pathological gambler." "If I start gambling I would never stop." "I would go right back into that addiction misery again." "I can go home and talk to my wife." "I can go for a walk." "I can meditate." "I can go to a 12-step meeting." "I can call my sponsor or spiritual leader and go out for a cup of coffee." "I can cope with this feeling." "If I just wait for 15 minutes, the craving will pass." "If I move away from the high-risk situation, I would feel better soon."

1. _____

2. _____

3. _____

4. _____

5. _____

6. _____

7. _____

8. _____

9. _____

10. _____

Write down these 10 alternative behaviors, and carry them with you. Remember that you have to practice these skills until they become automatic. Practice saying and doing these things with your group, counselor, sponsor, mentor, coach, spouse, friend, or 12-step member. Practice, practice, practice until you feel comfortable with the new skill.

You need to check warning signs daily in your personal inventory. You also need to have other people check you daily. You will not always pick up the symptoms in yourself. You might be denying the problem again. Your spouse, your sponsor, and/or a fellow 12-step member can warn you when they believe that you might be in trouble. Listen to these people. If they tell you that they sense a problem, then take action. You might need professional help in working the problem through. Do not hesitate to call and ask for help. Anything is better than relapsing. If you overreact to a warning sign, you are not going to be in trouble. If you under react, you might be headed for real problems. Addiction is a deadly disease. Your life is at stake.

High-Risk Situations

Relapse is more likely to occur in certain situations. These situations can trigger relapse. People relapse when faced with high-risk situations that they could not cope with except by gambling. For a while it is best that you cancel all of your credit and ATM cards and have someone else manage your money. Designate a person to cosign every check and bank withdrawal. Plan activities other than gambling on payday. Only carry with you the bare minimum amount of money you will need each day. Money is a trigger. Your job in treatment is to develop coping skills for dealing with each high-risk situation.

Negative Emotions

Many people relapse when feeling negative feelings that they cannot cope with. Most feel angry or frustrated, but some feel anxious, bored, lonely, or depressed.

Almost any negative feeling can lead to relapse if you do not learn how to cope with the feeling. Feelings motivate you to take action. You must act to solve any problem. Circle any of the following feelings that seem to lead you to gamble.

1. Loneliness

2. Anger

3. Rejection

4. Emptiness

5. Annoyed

6. Sad

7. Exasperated

8. Betrayed

9. Cheated

10. Frustrated

11. Envious

12. Exhausted

13. Bored

14. Anxious

15. Ashamed

16. Bitter

17. Burdened

18. Foolish

19. Jealous

20. Left out

21. Selfish

22. Restless

23. Weak

24. Sorrowful

25. Greedy

26. Aggravated

27. Manipulated

28. Miserable

29. Unloved

30. Worried

31. Scared

32. Spiteful

33. Sorrowful

34. Helpless

35. Neglected

36. Grief

37. Confused

38. Crushed

39. Discontented

40. Restless

41. Irritated

42. Overwhelmed

43. Panicked

44. Trapped

45. Unsure

46. Intimidated

47. Distraught

48. Uneasy

49. Guilty

50. Threatened

A Plan to Deal With Negative Emotions

These are just a few of the feeling words. Add more if you need to do so. Develop coping skills for dealing with each feeling that makes you vulnerable to relapse. Exactly what are you going to do when you have this feeling? Detail your specific plan of action. Some options are talking to your sponsor, calling a friend in the program, going to a meeting, calling your counselor, reading some recovery material, turning it over to your Higher Power, and getting some exercise. For each feeling, develop a specific plan of action.

Feeling _____

    Plan 1. _____

    Plan 2. _____

    Plan 3. _____

Feeling _____

    Plan 1. _____

    Plan 2. _____

    Plan 3. _____

Feeling _____

    Plan 1. _____

    Plan 2. _____

    Plan 3. _____

Continue to fill out these feeling forms until you have all of the feelings that give you trouble and you have coping skills for dealing with each feeling.

Social Pressure

Social pressure can be direct (where someone directly encourages you to gamble) or indirect (a social situation where people are gambling). Both of these situations can trigger intense craving, and this can lead to relapse.

Certain friends are more likely to encourage you to gamble. These people do not want to hurt you. They want you to relax and have a good time. They want their old friend back. They do not understand the nature of your disease. Perhaps they are problem gamblers themselves and are in denial.

High-Risk Friends

Make a list of the friends who might encourage you to gamble.

1. _____

2. _____

3. _____

4. _____

5. _____

What are you going to do when they ask you to come with them to gamble? What are you going to say? In skills group, set up a situation where the whole group encourages you to gamble. Look carefully at how you feel when the group members are encouraging you. Look at what you say. Have them help you to develop appropriate ways of saying no. The skills of saying no are the following:

- Look at the person and say no thank you.
- Suggest another alternative behavior.

- If the person persists, tell them that you are trying to stop behavior that has been harming you. Then ask them to help you by respecting your choice not to use.
- If they persist, leave the situation. "Well, I have got to be going. Nice to see you."

High-Risk Social Situations

Certain social situations will trigger craving. These are the situations where you have gambled in the past. Casinos, bars or restaurants with video lottery machines, service stations with video lottery terminals, a particular part of town, certain music, athletic events, parties, weddings, family events—all of these situations can trigger intense cravings. Make a list of five social situations where you will be vulnerable to relapse.

1. _____

2. _____

3. _____

4. _____

5. _____

Early on in your recovery, you will need to avoid these situations and friends. To put yourself in a high-risk situation is asking for trouble. If you have to attend a function where there will be people gambling, then take someone with you who is in the program. Take someone with you who will support you in your recovery. Make sure that you have a way to get home. You do not have to stay and torture yourself. You can leave if you feel uncomfortable. Avoid all situations where your recovery feels shaky.

Interpersonal Conflict

Many addicts relapse when in a conflict with some other person. They have a problem with someone and have no idea of how to cope with conflict so they might revert to old behavior and use the addiction to deal with the uncomfortable feelings. The stress of the problem builds and leads to gambling. This conflict usually happens with someone who they are closely involved with—wife, husband, child, parent, sibling, friend, boss, and so on.

You can have a serious problem with anyone—even a stranger—so you must have a plan for dealing with interpersonal conflict. You will develop specific skills in treatment that will help you to communicate even when you are under stress.

You need to learn and practice the following interpersonal skills repeatedly.

1. Tell the truth all of the time.

2. Share how you feel.

3. Ask for what you want.

4. Find some truth in what the other person is saying.

5. Be willing to compromise.

If you can stay in the conflict and work it out, that is great. If you cannot, then you have to leave the situation and take care of yourself. You might have to go for a walk, a run, or a drive. You might need to cool down. You must stop the conflict. You cannot continue to try to deal with a situation that you believe is too much for you. Do not feel bad about this. Interpersonal relationships are the hardest challenge we face. Carry a card with you that lists the telephone numbers of people who you can contact. You might want to call your sponsor, minister, counselor, a fellow GA member, friend, family member, doctor, or anyone else who may support you.

In an interpersonal conflict, you will fear abandonment. You need to get accurate and reassure yourself that people can disagree with you and still care about you. Remember that your Higher Power cares about you. A Higher Power created you and loves you. Remember the other people in your life who love you. This is one of the main reasons for talking with someone else. When the other person listens to you, that person gives you the feeling that you are accepted and loved.

If you still feel afraid or angry, then get with someone you trust and stay with that person until you feel safe. Do not struggle out there all by yourself. Any member of your 12-step group will understand how you are feeling. We all have had these problems. We all have felt lost, helpless, hopeless, and angry.

Make an emergency card that lists all of the people who you can call if you are having difficulty. Write down their phone numbers, and carry this card with you at all times. Show this card to your counselor. Practice asking someone for help in treatment once each day. Write down the situation and show it to your counselor. Get into the habit of asking for help. When you get out of treatment, call someone every day just to stay in touch and keep the lines of communication open. Get used to it. Do not wait to ask for help at the last minute. This makes asking more difficult.

Positive Feelings

Some people relapse when they are feeling positive emotions. Think of all the times you used gambling to celebrate. That has gotten to be such a habit that when something good happens, you will immediately think about gambling. You need to be ready when you feel like a winner. This may be when you are out of town, get a promotion, or any event where you feel good. How are you going to celebrate without gambling? Make a celebration plan. You might have to take someone with you to a celebration, particularly in early recovery.

Positive feelings also can work when you are by yourself. A beautiful spring day can be enough to get you thinking about gambling. You need an action plan for when these thoughts pass through your mind. You must immediately get accurate and get real. In recovery, we are committed to reality. Do not sit there and recall how wonderful you will feel if you gamble. Tell yourself the truth. Think about all of the pain that addiction has caused you. If you toy with positive feelings, then you ultimately will gamble.

Circle the positive feelings that may make you vulnerable to relapse.

1. Affection
2. Boldness
3. Braveness
4. Calmness
5. Capableness
6. Cheerfulness
7. Confidence
8. Delightfulness
9. Desire
10. Enchantment
11. Joy
12. Freeness
13. Gladness
14. Glee
15. Happiness
16. Honor
17. Horny
18. Infatuation
19. Inspired
20. Kinky
21. Lazy
22. Loving
23. Peaceful
24. Pleasant
25. Pleased
26. Sexy
27. Wonderful
28. Cool
29. Relaxed
30. Reverent
31. Silly
32. Vivacious
33. Adequate
34. Efficient
35. Successful
36. Accomplished

37. Hopeful

38. Cheery

39. Elated

40. Merry

41. Ecstatic

42. Upbeat

43. Splendid

44. Yearning

45. Bliss

46. Excitement

47. Exhilaration

48. Proudness

49. Aroused

50. Festive

Plan to Cope With Positive Feelings

These are the feelings that may make you vulnerable to relapse. You must be careful when you are feeling good because pleasure triggers the same part of the brain that triggers addiction. Make an action plan for dealing with each positive emotion that makes you vulnerable to gamble.

Feeling _____

　　　　　　Plan 1. _____

　　　　　　Plan 2. _____

　　　　　　Plan 3. _____

Feeling _____

　　　　　　Plan 1. _____

　　　　　　Plan 2. _____

　　　　　　Plan 3. _____

Feeling _____

　　　　　　Plan 1. _____

　　　　　　Plan 2. _____

　　　　　　Plan 3. _____

Continue this planning until you develop a plan for each of the positive feelings that make you vulnerable. Practice what you are going to do when you experience positive feelings.

Test Control

Some people gamble to test whether they can gamble safely again. They fool themselves into thinking that they might be able to gamble normally. This time they will gamble only a little. This time they will be able to stay in control of themselves. People who fool themselves this way are in for big trouble. From the first use, most people are in full-blown relapse within 30 days.

Testing personal control begins with inaccurate thinking. It takes you back to Step One. You need to think accurately. You are powerless over gambling. If you use, then you will lose. It is as simple as that. You are physiologically, psychologically, and socially addicted. The cells in your body will not suddenly change, no matter how long you are in recovery. You are addicted in your cells. There are physical highways in the brain that will always think inaccurately that you can gamble safely.

How to See Through the First Bet

You need to look at how the illness part of yourself will try to convince you that you are not a pathological gambler. The illness will flash on the screen of your consciousness all the good things that the addiction did for you. Make a list of these things. In the first column, marked "Early Gambling," write down some of the good things that you were getting out of gambling. Why were you using? What good came out of it? Did it make you feel social, smart, pretty, intelligent, brave, popular, desirable, relaxed, or sexy? Did it help you to sleep? Did it make you feel confident? Did it help you to forget your problems? Make a long list. These are the good things that you were getting when you first started using. This is why you were using.

Early Gambling	Late Gambling
1.	1.
2.	2.
3.	3.
4.	4.
5.	5.
6.	6.
7.	7.
8.	8.
9.	9.
10.	10.

Now go back and place in the second column, marked "Late Gambling," how you were doing in that area once you became addicted. How were you doing in that same area right before you came into treatment? Did you still feel social, or did you feel alone? Did you still feel intelligent, or did you feel stupid? You will find that a great change has taken place. The very things that you were using for in early use, you get the opposite of in late use. If you were gambling for relaxation, then you cannot relax. If you were gambling to be more popular, then you are more isolated, insecure, and alone. If you were gambling to feel powerful, then you are feeling more afraid. This is a major characteristic of addiction. The good things you got at first you get the opposite of in addiction. You can never go back to early use because your brain has permanently changed in chemistry, structure, and genetics.

Take a long look at both of these lists, and think about how the illness is going to try to work inside of your thinking. The addicted part of yourself will present to you all of the good things you got in early gambling. This is how the disease will encourage you to gamble. You must see through the first gambling to the consequences that are dead ahead.

Look at that second list. You must see the misery that is coming if you gamble. For most people who relapse, there are only a few days of controlled use before loss of control sets in. There usually are only a few hours or days before all of the bad stuff begins to click back into place. Relapse is terrible. It is the most intense misery that you can imagine.

Lapse and Relapse

A lapse is the use of any addictive behavior. A relapse is continuing to use the behavior until the full biological, psychological, and social disease is present. All of the complex biological, psychological, and social components of the disease become evident very quickly.

The Lapse Plan

You must have a plan in case you lapse. It is foolish to think that you never will have a problem again. You must plan what you are going to do if you have a problem. Hunt et al. (1971), in a study of recovering addicts, found that 33% of clients lapsed within 2 weeks of leaving treatment, and 60% lapsed within 3 months. At the end of 8 months, 63% had lapsed. At the end of 12 months, 67% had lapsed.

The worst thing you can do when you have a lapse is to think that you have completely failed in recovery. This is inaccurate thinking. You are not a total failure. You have not lost everything. A lapse is a great learning opportunity. You have made a mistake, and you can learn from it. You let some part of your program go, and you are paying for it. You need to examine exactly what happened and get back into recovery.

A lapse is an emergency. It is a matter of life or death. You must take immediate action to prevent the lapse from becoming a full relapse. You must call someone in the program—preferably your sponsor—and tell that person what happened. You need to examine why you had a problem. You cannot use the addiction and the tools of recovery at the same time. Something went wrong. You did not use your new skills. You must make a plan of action to recover from your lapse. You cannot do this by yourself. You are in denial. You do not know the whole truth. If you did, you would not have relapsed.

Call your sponsor or a professional counselor, and have that person develop a new treatment plan for you. You may need to attend more meetings. You may need to see a counselor. You may need outpatient treatment. You may need inpatient treatment. You have to get honest with yourself. You need to develop a plan and follow it. You need someone else to agree to keep an eye on you for a while. Do not try to do this alone. What we cannot do alone, we can do together.

THE BEHAVIOR CHAIN

All behavior occurs in a certain sequence. First there is the *trigger*. This is the external event that starts the behavioral sequence. After the trigger, there comes *thinking*. Much of this thinking is very fast, and you will not consciously pick it up unless you stop and think about it. The thoughts trigger *feeling*, which gives you energy and direction for action. Next comes the *behavior* or the action initiated by the trigger. Lastly, there always is a *consequence* for any action.

Diagrammed, the behavior chain looks like this:

Trigger → Thinking → Feeling → Behavior → Consequence

Let us go through a behavioral sequence and see how it works. On the way home from work, Mark, a recovering gambler, passes a local casino. (This is the trigger.) He thinks, "I have had a hard day. I would make a couple of bets to unwind." (The trigger initiates thinking.) Mark craves gambling. (The thinking initiates feeling.) Mark turns into the casino and begins gambling. (The feeling initiates behavior.) Mark loses all of his money, including his next month's mortgage payment. (The behavior has a consequence.)

Let us work through another example. It is 11:00 pm, and Mark is not asleep (trigger). He thinks, "I would never get to sleep tonight unless I make a few bets on the Internet" (thinking). He feels an increase in his anxiety about not sleeping (feeling). He gets up and gambles online. He stops after going into debt on all of his credit cards and wakes up unable to work the next morning (consequence).

How to Cope With Triggers

At every point along the behavior chain, you can work on preventing relapse. First you need to examine your triggers. What environmental events lead you to gambling? We went over some of these when we examined high-risk situations. Determine what people, places, or things make you vulnerable to relapse. Stay away from these triggers as much as possible. If a trigger occurs, then use your new coping skills.

Do not let the trigger initiate old behavior. Stop and think. Do not let your thinking get out of control. Challenge your thinking and get accurate about what is real. Let us look at some common inaccurate thoughts.

1. One bet is not going to hurt.

2. No one is going to know.

3. I need to relax.

4. I am just going to place a few bets.

5. I have had a hard day.

6. My friends want me to gamble. It is fun.

7. I never had a problem with poker.

8. It is the only way I can sleep.

9. I can do anything I want to.

10. I am lonely.

All of these inaccurate thoughts can be used to fuel the craving that leads to relapse. You must stop and challenge your thinking until you are thinking accurately. You must replace inaccurate thoughts with accurate ones. You are a pathological gambler. If you gamble, you will lose everything. That is the truth. Think through the first drink. Get honest with yourself.

How to Cope With Craving

If you think inaccurately, then you will begin craving. This is the powerful feeling that drives compulsive gambling. Craving is like an ocean wave; it will build and then wash over you. Craving does not last long if you move away from your addiction. If you move closer to the addiction, then the craving will increase until you are compelled to gamble. Immediately on feeling a desire to gamble, think this thought:

"Gambling is no longer an option for me."

Now gambling is no longer is an option. What are your options? You are in trouble. You are craving. What are you going to do to prevent relapse? You must move away from gambling thoughts and behaviors and choose what is accurate. Perhaps you need to call your sponsor, go to a meeting, turn it over, call the GA hotline, call the treatment center, call your counselor, go for a walk, run, or visit someone. You must do something else other than thinking about chemicals. Do not sit there and ponder gambling. You will lose that debate. This illness is called the great debater. If you leave it unchecked, it will seduce you into gambling.

Remember that the illness must lie to work. You must uncover the lie as quickly as possible and get back to the truth. You must take the appropriate action necessary to maintain your recovery.

A DAILY RELAPSE PREVENTION PLAN

If you work a daily program of recovery, then your chances of success increase greatly. You need to evaluate your recovery daily and keep a log. This is your daily inventory.

1. Assess all relapse warning signs.

    a. What symptoms did I see in myself today?

    b. What am I going to do about them?

2. Assess love of self.

    a. What did I do to love myself today?

    b. What am I going to do tomorrow?

3. Assess love of others.

    a. What did I do to love others today?

    b. What am I going to do tomorrow?

4. Assess love of God.

    a. What did I do to love God today?

    b. What am I going to do tomorrow?

5. Assess sleep pattern.

    How am I sleeping?

6. Assess exercise.

    Am I getting enough exercise?

7. Assess nutrition.

    Am I eating right?

8. Review total recovery program.

    a. How am I doing in recovery?

    b. What is the next step in my recovery program?

9. Read GA material.

10. Make conscious contact with God.

    a. Pray and meditate for a few minutes.

    b. Relax completely.

Social Support System

Every client needs to build a social support system. Positive social support is highly predictive of long-term abstinence rates across many addictive behaviors. You need to write down specifically who is going to be your advocate at home, work, community, and school. This person needs to talk to your counselor and understand exactly what being an advocate means. This person will have different tasks depending upon whether or not they are a schoolteacher, parent, spouse, pastor, sponsor, mentor, coach, community leader, school counselor, doctor, nurse, counselor, etc. You need to make a list of all of these people and decide who is going to do what. Someone needs to check up on you every day. You will need to cancel all credit cards and give all of your extra money to someone you trust. Limit your ability to write a check by having to have a cosigner to write checks. Many gambling casinos have a self-exclusion program where you can sign a contract that will allow them to prevent you from gambling in their establishment. You will have to talk to security; they will take your picture and sign the no gambling contract with you. The contract can last as long as you like, but 5 years is a good length.

PEOPLE WHO CAN HELP YOU IN RECOVERY

1. Case Manager: _____ Phone: _____

The continuing care case manager makes sure everyone on the team is working together to keep the client free from gambling. This person keeps a record of all therapy meetings and 12-step groups. They have a contract with the client that outlines exactly what is expected of the client and what the consequences are if the client does not follow through with the recovery program.

2. Parent or Spouse: _____ Phone: _____

The parent or spouse will be the person who knows what behavior is adaptive and maladaptive. What friends are to be avoided? If an adolescent develops the behavioral contract, he or she is responsible for rewards and consequences.

3. The Teacher: _____ Phone: _____

4. Employer: _____ Phone: _____

5. Sponsor\Mentor\Coach: _____ Phone: _____

The sponsor\mentor\coach is the person who guides the client through recovery. They are in a 12-step program themselves and take the client to meetings and meet regularly to discuss the recovery process.

Each person knows about what behavior is to be expected and what is not to be tolerated. Members of the team often call each other to check up on the facts and make sure everyone is on the same page.

6. The Physician: _____ Phone: _____

The physician orders the medication and does history and physical examinations to maintain good health.

7. The Spiritual Guide: _____ Phone: _____

The spiritual guide helps the client discuss and grow in his or her spiritual journey. The client shares his or her spiritual journey and maybe keeps a spiritual prayer journal.

8. Money Manager: _____ Phone: _____

The money manager manages the client's money, cosigns checks, arranges for daily allowance, makes sure paychecks are direct deposited, and makes sure all credit cards and ATM cards are canceled.

Fill out this inventory every day following treatment, and keep a journal about how you are doing. You will be amazed as you read back over your journal from time to time. You will be surprised at how much you have grown.

Make a list of 10 reasons why you want to stop gambling.

1. _____

2. _____

3. _____

4. _____

5. _____

6. _____

7. _____

8. _____

9. _____

10. _____

Never forget these reasons. Read this list over and over to yourself. Carry a copy with you and memorize them. If you are struggling in sobriety, then take it out and read it to yourself. You are important. No one has to live a life of misery. You can recover and live a clean and sober life.

I am in the _____.

_____ Precontemplation stage

_____ Contemplation stage

_____ Preparation stage

_____ Action stage

_____ Maintenance stage

Personal Recovery Plan

Name: _____ Home Phone: _____

Admission Date: _____ Work Phone: _____

Discharge Date: _____ Phone: _____

Name of Significant Other: _____

It is important to your recovery to continue to work through your problems on discharge. Your recovery never can stand still. You must be constantly moving forward in your program. Working with your counselor, you must detail exactly what you need to do following inpatient treatment. Each psychological problem or family problem will need a specific plan of action. You must commit yourself to following this recovery plan to the letter. Do not think that just because you have completed treatment that your problems are over. Your recovery is just beginning, and you need to work diligently to stay clean and sober.

Make a list of the problems that you need to address in continuing care. Any emotional, family, legal, social, physical, leisure, work, spiritual, or school problem will have to have a plan. How are you going to address that problem in recovery? What is the goal? What do you want to achieve? Develop your personal recovery plan with your counselor's assistance.

A. Treatment plan for continued recovery

    1. Problem 1: _____

       Goal: _____

       Plan: _____

       _____

       _____

2. Problem 2: _____

   Goal: _____

   Plan: _____

   _____

   _____

3. Problem 3: _____

   Goal: _____

   Plan: _____

   _____

   _____

4. Problem 4: _____

   Goal: _____

   Plan: _____

   _____

   _____

5. Problem 5: _____

   Goal: _____

   Plan: _____

   _____

   _____

B. Relapse

In the event of a relapse, list five steps that you will take to deal with the problem.

1. _____

2. _____

3. _____

4. _____

5. _____

C. Support in recovery

Indicate the 12-step meetings that you will attend each week after discharge. We recommend that you attend 90 meetings in 90 days at first and at least 3 to 5 meetings per week for the remainder of that year, and then you can attend once a week for at least the next 5 years.

Day _____

Time _____

Location _____

D. Indicate when you will attend the continuing care group.

Day _____

Time _____

Location _____

E. Who are three 12-step contact persons who can provide you with support in early recovery?

Name: _____ Phone: _____

Name: _____ Phone: _____

Name: _____ Phone: _____

F. If you have any problems or concerns in sobriety, you always can call the treatment center staff at the following number:

Counselor: _____

Phone: _____

G. If you and your counselor have arranged for further counseling or treatment following discharge, then complete the following:

Name of Agency: _____

Address: _____ Phone: _____

First Appointment:_____

Day _____

Time_____

H. List 10 things that you are going to do daily to stay in recovery.

1. _____

2. _____

3. _____

4. _____

5. _____

6. _____

7. _____

8. _____

9. _____

10. _____

I. You are changing your lifestyle. It will be important to avoid certain people and situations that will put you at high risk. List 10 people and places you need to avoid in early recovery.

1. _____

2. _____

3. _____

4. _____

5. _____

6. _____

7. _____

8. _____

9. _____

10. _____

You will need a series of advocates who know your story and commitment to recovery. You sign a release with each of these people so they can talk to each other about your recovery. It helps to have someone at home, work, school, and community. List their names and numbers, contact them, and ask them to be an advocate for you in your community.

- Home Advocate:

    Person:_____Phone:_____Address:_____

    _____

    _____

- School Advocate:

    Person:_____Phone:_____Address:_____

    _____

    _____

- Work Advocate:

  Person:_____Phone:_____Address:_____

  _____

  _____

- Community Advocate:

  Person:_____Phone:_____Address:_____

  _____

  _____

- Case Manager:

  Person:_____Phone:_____Address:_____

  _____

  _____

You will call the case manager every day to see if this is a day for you to come in for drug testing. You will get up to three drug tests per week for the first 6 months and up to one drug test for the next 5 years. You will send in a monthly log of 12-step meetings to your case manager by the 10th of each month. Each meeting has to be dated and signed by the meeting leader. The case manager will receive reports from all of the treatment that was recommended by the treatment center, such as anger management, marriage counseling, etc. You will sign a contract with the case manager that gives consequences if you do not follow the continuing care program. This will mean the manager will contact your boss, probation officer, family members, licensing board, or another person or agency that is dedicated to your successful treatment.

STATEMENT OF COMMITMENT

I understand that the success of my recovery depends on adherence to my recovery plan. The continuing care program has been explained to me, and I understand fully what I must do in recovery. I commit to myself that I will follow this plan.

With your continuing care manager, write out your continuing care plan and then have all mentors/sponsors/coaches and advocates sign it.

Client Signature: _____

Physician Signature: _____

Sponsor Signature: _____

Employer Signature: _____

Significant Other Signature: _____

Licensing Board Signature: _____

Community Advocate Signature: _____

School Advocate Signature: _____

Case Manager Signature: _____

Counselor Signature: _____

Date: _____

Stress Management

Unresolved stress fuels addiction. Addicted individuals deal with stress by using chemicals or addictive behavior rather than using other, more appropriate coping skills. Everyone has stress, and everyone needs to learn how to cope with stress in daily life. Stress is the generalized physiological response to a stressor. A stressor is any demand made on the body.

A stressor can be anything that mobilizes the body for change. This can include psychological or physiological loss, absence of stimulation, excessive stimulation, frustration of an anticipated reward, conflict, and presentation or anticipation of painful events (Zegans, 1982).

The stress response is good and adaptive. It activates the body for problem solving. Stress is destructive only when it is chronic. The overly stressed body produces harmful chemicals such as cortisol that triggers inflammation, and soon the person gets sick. Initially, the body produces certain chemicals to handle the stressful situation. Initially, these chemical changes are adaptive. In the end, they are destructive. Severe or chronic stress has been linked to irreversible disease including kidney impairment, hypertension, arteriosclerosis, type 2 diabetes, ulcers, and a compromised immune system that can result in increased infections and cancer (Selye, 1956).

When animals encounter an unsolvable problem, they ultimately get sick. They fall victim to a wide variety of physical and mental disorders. Under chronic stress, these organisms ultimately die.

It seems that everyone has a genetic predisposition to break down in a certain organ system when under chronic stress. Some people get depressed; some get ulcers, heart attacks, strokes, and some become chemically dependent.

In treatment, you must learn how to deal with stress in ways other than by using your addiction. You must learn to use the stress signals that your body gives you to help you solve problems. If you cannot solve the problem yourself, then you need to get some help.

Most people who are addicted are dealing with unresolved pain. They begin drinking, gambling, or using chemicals to ease the pain, and soon they become dependent. Addiction is a primary disease. It takes over people's lives and makes everything worse.

Stress management techniques help addicted individuals to regain the control they have lost in their lives. By establishing and maintaining a daily program of recovery, they learn how to cope with stress. If you are dealing with stress better, then you are not as likely to relapse. There are three elements necessary to reduce your overall stress level: (1) a regular exercise program, (2) regular relaxation, and (3) creating a more rewarding lifestyle.

RELAXATION

For centuries, people have relaxed or used meditation to quiet their minds and reach a state of peace. When animals have enough to eat and they are safe, they lay down. People do not do that because humans are the only animals that worry about the future. Humans fear that if they relax today, then they will be in trouble tomorrow.

Benson (1975, 2000) showed that when people relax twice a day for 10 to 20 minutes, it has a major impact on their overall stress levels. People who do this have fewer illnesses, feel better, and are healthier. Illness such as high blood pressure, ulcers, and headaches can go away completely with a regular relaxation program.

Benson maintained that the relaxation technique is simple.

1. Sit or lie down in a quiet place.

2. Pay attention to your breathing.

3. Every time you exhale, say the word *one* over quietly to yourself. It is normal for other ideas to come, but when they do, just return to the word or words you have chosen.

4. Do this for 10 to 20 minutes twice a day.

You do not have to use the word *one*. You can use any other word or phrase of your choice, but it has to be the same word or phrase repeated over and over again. You can get some relaxation tapes or music that you find relaxing. You can pray or meditate. The most important thing is to relax as completely as you can. If you do

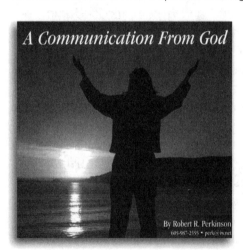

this, then your stress level will be lower and you will be better able to mobilize yourself to deal with stress when it occurs. I have created a meditation exercise CD that you might find helpful. You can find this at www.cdbaby.com/cd/godtalks2. This tape has two tracks. Track 1 is a 20-minute spiritual exercise followed by relaxing music. Track 2 is a 12-minute meditation exercise followed by relaxing music. Many of our clients find this to be the turning point in their spiritual connection because it is the first time they experience the presence of God.

Progressive relaxation is tightening each muscle group and then relaxing them. For example, you tighten your right arm and feel the tension. Then let the muscle go and feel it deeply relax. Concentrate on the feeling of tension and relaxation. Soon you will not have to tighten the muscle group as often you will just have to concentrate on it relaxing. As you practice relaxation, you will learn how it feels to be relaxed. Try to keep this feeling all day long.

- When you feel stressed, stop and take two deep breaths.
- Breathe in through your nose and out through your mouth.
- As you exhale, feel a warm wave of relaxation flow down your body.

- Once you have regained your state of relaxation, return to your day and move a little slower this time.
- Remember, nothing is ever done too well or too slowly. You do not have to do things quickly to succeed.

When you come to some new task that you think you have to complete, ask yourself several important questions.

1. Do I have to do this?

_____

_____

_____

_____

_____

2. Do I have to do it now?

_____

_____

_____

_____

_____

3. Is this going to make a difference in 5 years?

_____

_____

_____

_____

_____

If the new stressor is not that important, perhaps you should not do it at all. Do not overly stress yourself. That does not make any sense. Know your limits. Achieve a state of relaxation in the morning, and listen to your body all day long. If anything threatens your serenity, turn it over and let God deal with it.

For the next week, set aside two times a day for relaxation. Go through the meditation exercise we discussed or some other relaxation exercise. Score the level of relaxation you achieved from 1 (*as little as possible*) to 100 (*as much as possible*). Then score your general stress level during the day in the same way. Write down any comments about your stress. List the situations when you felt the most tension.

Day 1

Relaxation Score

Daily Stress Score

Comments

Day 2

Relaxation Score

Daily Stress Score

Comments

Day 3

Relaxation Score

Daily Stress Score

Comments

Day 4

Relaxation Score

Daily Stress Score

Comments

Day 5

Relaxation Score

Daily Stress Score

Comments

Day 6

Relaxation Score

Daily Stress Score

Comments

Day 7

Relaxation Score

Daily Stress Score

Comments

EXERCISE

The role of exercise in the treatment of addiction has been well established. Significant improvements in physical fitness can occur in as short a period as 20 days. People who maintain a regular exercise program feel less depressed and less anxious, improve their self-concepts, and enhance the quality of their lives (Folkins & Sime, 1981).

Most addicted people come into treatment in poor physical and mental shape. They gave up on exercise a long time ago. Even if they were in good physical condition at one time in their lives, the addiction has taken its toll. These people are unable to maintain a consistent level of physical fitness. The mind and body cannot maintain a regular exercise program when a person chronically abuses drugs, alcohol, or other addictive behaviors.

An exercise program, although difficult to develop, can be fun. You get a natural high from exercise that you do not get in any other way. It feels good, and it feels good all day.

A good exercise program includes three elements: (1) stretching, (2) strength, and (3) cardiovascular fitness. The recreational therapist or personal trainer will assist you in developing an individualized program specific to you.

Stretching means that you increase a muscle's range of motion until you become supple and flexible. Never stretch your muscles to the point of pain. The body will warn you well before you go too far. Let the exercise therapist show you how to stretch each major muscle group. Get into a habit of stretching before all exercise.

In a strength program, you gradually lift more weight until you become stronger. Do not lift more often than every other day. The muscles need a full day of rest to repair them. Soon you can increase the load. Three sets of 8 to 12 repetitions each is a standard exercise for each muscle group. The exercise therapist will show you how to complete each exercise. Correct technique is very important.

Endurance training means that you exercise at a training heart rate for an extended period of time. This is where the cardiovascular system gets stronger. Your training heart rate is calculated by taking your age, minus the number 220, multiplied by .75.

Cardiovascular fitness is attained when you exercise at a training heart rate, for 20 to 30 minutes, at least three times a week. Have the exercise therapist help you to determine your training heart rate and develop a program in which you gradually increase your cardiovascular fitness. Usually, you will be increasing your exercise by 10% each week.

Many forms of exercise can be beneficial for cardiovascular training. The key point is this: It must be sustained exercise for at least 20 to 30 minutes. Walking is probably the best exercise to start with. It is easy to do, and you do not need any specialized equipment. The exercise cannot be a stop–start exercise such as tennis or golf. It must be something that you can sustain. These include exercises such as walking, jogging, swimming, and biking.

After you have worked out your exercise program, keep a daily log of your exercise. Reinforce yourself when you reach one of your goals. You might have a goal of running a mile by the end of the month. If you reach your goal, then buy yourself something you want or treat yourself to a movie to celebrate. Write down your exercise schedule for the next month.

EXERCISE PROGRAM

Date   *Training Heart Rate*

Strength

Stretching

Cardiovascular fitness

CHANGING YOUR LIFESTYLE

Along with maintaining a regular relaxation and exercise time, you must change other aspects of your life to improve your stress management skills.

Problem Solving Skills

You need to be able to identify and respond to the problems in your life. Unsolved problems increase your stress level. Problems are a normal part of life, and you need specific skills to deal with them effectively. For each problem that you encounter, work through the following steps:

1. Identify the problem.

2. Clarify your goals. What do you want?

3. Consider all the alternatives of action.

4. Think through each alternative, eliminating one at a time, until you have the best alternative.

5. Act on the problem.

6. Evaluate the effect of your action.

Work through several problems with your counselor or group while in treatment. See how effective it is to seek the advice and counsel of others. You need to ask for help.

Developing Pleasurable Activities

One of the things that gamblers fear the most is not being able to have fun when clean and sober. Gambling has been involved in pleasurable activities for so long that it is directly equated with all pleasure. To look forward to a life without being able to have fun is intolerable.

You do not give up fun in sobriety. You change the way in which you have fun. You cannot use gambling for pleasure anymore. This is not good for you. You can enjoy many pleasant activities without gambling. If you think about it, this is real fun anyway. The fun you are missing is based on a false feeling. Once you see how much fun you can have when clean and sober, you will be amazed.

Increasing pleasurable activities will elevate your mood and decrease your overall stress level. If you are not feeling well in recovery, it is likely that you are not involved in enough pleasurable activities. If you increase the level of pleasure, then you will feel better and be less vulnerable to relapse.

First, identify the things that you might enjoy doing, and then make a list of the things that you are going to do more often. Make a list of the activities that you plan to do for yourself each day. Write down your plan. The more pleasurable things you do, the better you will feel.

1. Being in the country
2. Wearing expensive clothes
3. Talking about sports
4. Meeting someone new
5. Going to a concert
6. Playing baseball or softball
7. Planning trips or vacations
8. Buying things for yourself
9. Going to the beach
10. Doing artwork
11. Rock climbing or mountaineering
12. Playing golf
13. Reading
14. Rearranging or redecorating your room or house
15. Playing basketball or volleyball
16. Going to a lecture
17. Breathing the clean air
18. Writing a song
19. Boating
20. Pleasing your parents
21. Watching television
22. Thinking quietly
23. Camping
24. Working on machines (e.g., cars, bikes, motors)

25. Working in politics

26. Thinking about something good in the future

27. Playing cards

28. Laughing

29. Working puzzles or crosswords

30. Having lunch with a friend or an associate

31. Playing tennis

32. Taking a bath

33. Going for a drive

34. Woodworking

35. Writing a letter

36. Being with animals

37. Riding in an airplane

38. Walking in the woods

39. Having a conversation with someone

40. Working at your job

41. Going to a party

42. Going to church functions

43. Visiting relatives

44. Going to a meeting

45. Playing a musical instrument

46. Having a snack

47. Taking a nap

48. Singing

49. Acting

50. Working on crafts

51. Being with your children

52. Playing a game of chess or checkers

53. Putting on makeup or fixing your hair

54. Visiting people who are sick or shut in

55. Bowling

56. Talking with your sponsor

57. Gardening or doing lawn work

58. Dancing

59. Sitting in the sun

60. Sitting and thinking

61. Praying

62. Meditating

63. Listening to the sounds of nature

64. Going on a date

65. Listening to the radio

66. Giving a gift

67. Reaching out to someone who is suffering

68. Getting or giving a massage or back rub

69. Talking to your spouse

70. Talking to a friend

71. Watching the clouds

72. Lying in the grass

73. Helping someone

74. Hearing or telling jokes

75. Going to church

76. Eating a good meal

77. Hunting

78. Fishing

79. Looking at the scenery

80. Working on improving your health

81. Going downtown

82. Watching a sporting event

83. Going to a health club

84. Learning something new

85. Horseback riding

86. Going out to eat

87. Talking on the telephone

88. Daydreaming

89. Going to the movies

90. Being alone

91. Feeling the presence of God

92. Smelling a flower

93. Looking at a sunrise

94. Doing a favor for a friend

95. Meeting a stranger

96. Reading the newspaper

97. Swimming

98. Walking barefoot

99. Playing catch or with a Frisbee

100. Cleaning your house or room

101. Listening to music

102. Knitting or crocheting

103. Having house guests

104. Being with someone you love

105. Having sexual relations

106. Going to the library

107. Watching people

108. Repairing something

109. Bicycling

110. Smiling at people

111. Caring for houseplants

112. Collecting things

113. Sewing

114. Going to garage sales

115. Water skiing

116. Surfing

117. Traveling

118. Teaching someone

119. Washing your car

120. Eating ice cream

Social Skills

What you do socially can turn people off or turn them on. If you do any of the following, you might be turning people off.

1. Not smiling

2. Failing to make eye contact

3. Not talking

4. Complaining

5. Telling everyone your troubles

6. Not responding to people

7. Whining

8. Being critical

9. Poor grooming

10. Not showing interest in people

11. Ignoring people

12. Having an angry look

13. Using nervous gestures

14. Feeling sorry for yourself

15. Always talking about the negative

You are turning people on if you do the following:

1. Smiling

2. Looking at people in the eyes

3. Expressing your concern

4. Talking about pleasant things

5. Being reinforcing

6. Telling people how nice they look

7. Being appreciative

8. Telling people that you care

9. Listening

10. Touching

11. Asking people to do something with you

12. Acting interested

13. Using people's names

14. Talking about the positive

15. Grooming yourself well

To have good social skills, you have to be assertive. You cannot be passive or aggressive. This means is that you have to tell people the truth about how you feel and ask for what you want. You must tell the truth at all times. If you withhold or distort information, then you never will be close to anyone.

Do not tell other people what to do; instead, ask them what they want to do. Do not let other people tell you what to do; instead, negotiate. Do not yell; instead, explain. Do not throw your weight around. When you are wrong, promptly admit it. Happiness is giving to others. The more you give, the more you get.

In a 12-step program, you never have to be alone. Your Higher Power always is with you. Learn to enjoy the presence of God, and communicate with God as if God were standing right beside you. Call someone in the program every day. Go to many meetings. Reach out to those who are still suffering. There are many people in jails or hospitals who need your help. Volunteer to work on the 12-step hotline. Ask people out for coffee after meetings. Do not worry if you are doing all of the asking at first. The reason you are doing this is for you. Most people, particularly men, feel very uncomfortable asking others to go out with them. Do not let that stop you. If you do not ask, then you will not have the experience of someone saying yes.

Using the pleasant activities list, make a plan for how you are going to increase your social interaction this month. Write all of it down, and reward yourself when you make progress. Here are a few hints to get you going:

1. Read the activities and entertainment section of your local newspaper. Mark down events that fit into your schedule and attend them.

2. Offer to become more involved in your 12-step group.

3. Ask the local chamber of commerce for information about groups and activities in the area.

4. Spend your weekends exploring new parts of town.

5. Smile.

6. Join another self-help support group such as an Adult Children of Alcoholics group or a singles group.

7. Join a church and get involved. Tell the pastor that you want to do something to help.

8. Volunteer your services with a local charity or hospital. Help others and share your experiences, strengths, and hopes.

9. Join a group that does interesting things in the area—hiking, skydiving, hunting, bird watching, acting, playing sports, joining a senior center, and so on. Check the local library for a list of such clubs and activities.

10. Ask someone in the program for interesting things to do in the area.

11. Go to an intergroup dance.

12. Go to an Alcoholics Anonymous (AA)/Narcotics Anonymous (NA) conference.

The most important thing to remember is that you are in recovery. You are starting a new life. To do this, you must take risks. You must reach out as you have never done before.

Appendix 1

Daily Craving Record

Rate your cravings every day on a scale of 0 (the least amount of craving possible) to 10 (the most craving possible). Then put down the situation or thoughts that triggered the craving. Have your counselor or group help you uncover the automatic thoughts or situations that triggered the craving. Do this at least for the first 90 days of recovery. Make as many copies of these pages that you need. In treatment, you will replace inaccurate thoughts with accurate thoughts.

0 = No craving 　　　　　　　3 = moderate craving 　　　　　　10 = severe craving

Date ___ Craving ___ Triggers _____

Date ___ Craving ___ Triggers _____

Date ___ Craving ___ Triggers _____

Date ___ Craving ___ Triggers _____

Date ___ Craving ___ Triggers _____

Date ___ Craving ___ Triggers _____

Date ___ Craving ___ Triggers _____

Date ___ Craving ___ Triggers _____

Date ___ Craving ___ Triggers _____

Date ___ Craving ___ Triggers _____

Date ___ Craving ___ Triggers _____

Date ___ Craving ___ Triggers _____

Date ___ Craving ___ Triggers _____

Date ___ Craving ___ Triggers _____

Date ___ Craving ___ Triggers _____

Date ___ Craving ___ Triggers _____

Date ___ Craving ___ Triggers _____

Date ___ Craving ___ Triggers _____

Date ___ Craving ___ Triggers _____

Date ___ Craving ___ Triggers _____

Date ___ Craving ___ Triggers _____

Date ___ Craving ___ Triggers _____

Date ___ Craving ___ Triggers _____

Date ___ Craving ___ Triggers _____

Date ___ Craving ___ Triggers _____

Date ___ Craving ___ Triggers _____

Date ___ Craving ___ Triggers _____

Date ___ Craving ___ Triggers _____

Date ___ Craving ___ Triggers _____

Date ___ Craving ___ Triggers _____

Date ___ Craving ___ Triggers _____

Date ___ Craving ___ Triggers _____

Date ___ Craving ___ Triggers _____

Date ___ Craving ___ Triggers _____

Appendix 2

Pressure Relief Group Meeting and Budget Form

TO THE GAMBLERS ANONYMOUS GROUP

When a member attends his or her first meeting, it is important that a pressure relief meeting be explained to him or her and that a member will contact him or her within 30 days to arrange a pressure relief meeting.

The member should be told to contact all creditors and tell them that he or she will be back to them in 30 days. It should be emphasized that no payments should be made and also that no commitment of dollar amounts should be promised. Each member should be told to choose someone to take care of his or her money (spouse, if married). It is suggested that the member's name be removed from all items of value (e.g., house, cars, stocks, bonds, bank books, credit cards, checking accounts). The member should be told not to carry more money than he or she needs for daily essentials.

The pressure relief meeting should be given only by a Gamblers Anonymous (GA) member experienced in pressure relief procedures. There should be at least one other GA member and a Gam-Anon member present. The pressure relief meeting should not take place at a member's home; there could be too many distractions. Do not plan a pressure relief meeting at a GA meeting room prior to a regularly scheduled meeting.

One week prior to the pressure relief meeting, the member should be given copies of the budget forms.

The pressure relief committee should schedule a reevaluation date approximately 6 months after the pressure relief meeting.

Dear Gamblers Anonymous Member:

According to the standards set forth by your local Gamblers Anonymous (GA) chapter, you are now eligible for a pressure group.

An integral part of your recovery is that of making financial restitution. Considering the fact that your debts usually are much greater than those of the average individual, it is vitally important that great care be taken when planning a manageable budget. The key word is *manageable*. It is very difficult for anyone to live a normal life while being overburdened with financial pressures, especially for a compulsive gambler.

The main concepts behind a compulsive gambler's pressure relief meeting are to allow the gambler and his or her family to be able to lead a normal life and, at the same time, make financial restitution to his or her creditors.

The first step in planning a budget requires total honesty. If you have withheld any information pertaining to your debts, now is the time to become totally honest. Hopefully, by now you have followed the advice of your fellow GA members and have done the following:

1. Contact all creditors and ask for a 30- to 45-day moratorium on payments. Be sure not to pay anyone, and do not make any financial commitments.

2. Choose someone to handle your money (spouse, if married).

3. Turn all ownership of properties (e.g., home, car) over to someone else.

4. Remove your name from all bank books, checking accounts, and credit cards.

5. Turn over all paychecks uncashed with stubs attached to the individual who will manage your money.

THE CHOICE IS YOURS

The choice between paying over a long period of time, while functioning and living as a human being, or complete collapse due to immense financial pressures that cannot be met is, in reality, not a choice at all but rather the only avenue that will return you back to sanity and solvency. You have to be honest, forthright, and humble in regard to the debts that you owe and in your determination to repay them. GA experience has shown that our creditors, in a very human and helpful way, will respond to sincerity, honesty, and courage but will rightfully reject arrogance and self-pity. Everyone is willing to help a person who is down (and who wants to get back up), but much more important is the willingness to help yourself. This is the key. This is the quest. This is the never-ending endeavor.

Have faith in the GA program, and follow the budget that will be set up for you. If you adhere to the budget and refrain from gambling, your financial pressures will soon be relieved, and this will greatly improve your chances for recovery. Remember that you have a gambling problem, not a financial problem. Go slowly; take it *one day at a time*.

DIRECTIONS

Please complete these pages with the most accurate and up-to-date information that you have available. Do not leave anything out.

TO THE CREDITOR

Dear Creditor:

The attached budget has been prepared for _____, who is a member of Gamblers Anonymous (GA). He/she has admitted that he/she is a compulsive gambler and that his/her life has become unmanageable. An integral part of the compulsive gambler's recovery is to make restitution to all of his/her creditors. Due to the fact that the compulsive gambler has accumulated a large debt, it may be necessary to repay you over a long period of time. If a previous repayment schedule already exists, the compulsive gambler may have to give you smaller payments and, therefore, take longer to repay his/her debt.

As you can see by the prepared budget, the compulsive gambler must provide for all living expenses for himself/herself and his/her family before paying his/her debts. The repayment schedule has been prepared by experienced members of GA. The amount suggested for repayment of each debt was based on the amount originally borrowed, the balance due, and the original monthly payment.

The compulsive gambler is not claiming bankruptcy and is not running away. He/she wants to repay his/her debts. Your cooperation is greatly appreciated.

GA is not responsible for the information listed on this form, nor does it guarantee the compliance of the proposed financial arrangement on this form.

Signed: _____

Pressure Relief Chairperson

Name: _____

Spouse's Name: _____

Date: _____

GA Group: _____

Budget Committee Chairperson: _____ Others: _____

Member's Phone:_____ Chairperson's Phone: _____

Reevaluation Date:_____

BUDGET

Expenses	Per Month[a]	Per Week
Alimony		
Allowance (children)		
Allowance (member)		
Allowance (spouse)		
Auto insurance		
Auto license		
Auto payment		
Auto registration		
Auto repairs		
Auto taxes/Tolls		
Babysitter		
Cable TV		
Car fare		
Child support/Day care		
Children's activities		
Christmas/Hanukkah gifts		
Cigarettes		
Clothing		
Coal/Wood/Kerosene		
Dentist		
Doctor		

Expenses	Per Month[a]	Per Week
Donations (e.g., church, temple, GA, Gam-Anon)		
Drugs and toiletries		
Dry cleaning and laundry		
Electricity		
Emergencies (e.g., home repairs)		
Eyeglasses/Contacts		
Family entertainment		
Film and developing		
Food		
GA conferences		
Garbage removal		
Gas (home)		
Gasoline (auto)		
Gifts (e.g., birthdays, anniversaries)		
Haircuts/Beauty salon		
Homeowner's/Renter's insurance		
Life insurance (term)		
Life-liner contribution		
Lunches (work)		
Medical insurance		
Mortgage (first)		
Mortgage (second)		
Mortgage (third)		
Music lessons		
Newspapers/Magazines		
Oil heat		
Pet care		
Postage		
Rent		
Savings/Retirement funds		
School tuition		
Taxes (income)		

(Continued)

(Continued)

Expenses	Per Month[a]	Per Week
Taxes (property)		
Telephone		
Therapy/Counseling		
Union/Club dues		
Vacation		
Water		
ITEMS NOT LISTED:		
TOTAL EXPENSES		

a. 4.33 weeks per month.

LIST OF CREDITORS

Please list, in the following order, (1) bad checks or debts for which you may be prosecuted, (2) court-ordered judgments, (3) credit unions, (4) bank or finance company loans, (5) back taxes, (6) credit cards, (7) bookmakers and loan sharks, (8) family and friends, and (9) others.

Creditor's Name	Date of Debt	Original Amount	Present Balance	Monthly Payment	Months in Default	Cosigner

REPAYMENT SCHEDULE

Creditor's Name	Original Balance	Balance	Monthly Payment	Weekly Payment	Date of First Payment	Estimated Date of Last Payment

FINANCIAL SUMMARY

Income	Per month		Child support Alimony		Property income	
	Per week				Spouse's income available	
	Primary job					
	Secondary job				Other income	
	Pensions				TOTAL	
Total Income:						
Subtract Total Expenses:						
Amount Available for Repayment:						

Gamblers Anonymous (GA) is not responsible for the information listed on this form, nor does it guarantee the compliance of the proposed financial arrangement on this form.

References

Burling, T. A., Reilly, P. M. Molten, J. O., & Ziff, D. C. (1989). Self-efficacy and relapse among inpatient drug and alcohol abusers: A predictor of outcome. *Journal of Studies on Alcohol, 50*(4), 354–360.

DiClemente, C. C. (2006). *Addiction and change: How addictions develop and addicted people recover.* New York: Guilford Press.

Frances, R. J., Bucky, S., & Alexopolos, G. S. (1984). Outcome study of familial and nonfamilial alcoholism. *American Journal of Psychiatry, 141*, 11.

Gamblers Anonymous. (1989a). *The combo book.* Los Angeles: G.A. Publishing.

Gamblers Anonymous. (1989b). *G.A.: A new beginning.* Los Angeles: G.A. Publishing.

Greenfield, S., Hufford, M., Vagge, L., Muenz, L., Costello, M., & Weiss, R. (2000). The relationship of self-efficacy expectations to relapse among alcohol dependent men and women: A prospective study. *Journal of Studies on Alcohol, 61*, 345–351.

Hunt, W. A., Barnett. L. W., & Branch, L. G. (1971). Relapse rates in addiction programs. *Journal of Clinical Psychology, 27*, 455–456.

Marlatt, A. G., & Donovan, D. M. (Eds.). (2008). *Relapse prevention: Maintenance strategies in the treatment of addictive behaviors.* New York: Guilford Press.

Marlatt, A. G., & Gordon, J. R. (1985). *Relapse prevention.* New York: Guilford Press.

Prochaska, J. O. (2003). Enhancing motivation to change. In A. W. Graham, T. K. Schultz, M. F. Mayo-Smith, & R. K. Ries (Eds.), *Principles of addiction medicine, third edition.* Chevy Chase, MD: American Society of Addiction Medicine, Inc.

Prochaska, J. O., & DiClemente, C. C. (1984). *The transtheoretical approach: Crossing the traditional boundries of therapy.* Malabar, FL: Krieger.

Shaffer, H. J., & LaPlante, D. A. (2008). Treatment of gambling disorders. In A.G. Marlatt & D. M. Donovan (Eds.), *Relapse prevention: Maintenance strategies in the treatment of addictive behaviors.* New York: Guilford Press.

About the Author

Robert R. Perkinson is the clinical director of Keystone Treatment Center in Canton, South Dakota. He is a licensed psychologist; licensed marriage & family therapist; internationally certified alcohol and drug counselor; South Dakota certified chemical dependency counselor, Level III; and a nationally certified gambling counselor and supervisor. His specialty areas focus on treating alcoholics, addicts, and pathological gamblers. He is the author of *Chemical Dependency Counseling: A Practical Guide* (2nd ed.) (2003a), which is the leading treatment manual in the world for chemical dependency counselors. With Dr. Arthur E. Jongsma Jr. (2001) he is the coauthor of *The Addiction Treatment Planner*, which is the best-selling treatment planner and computer software program for mental health and addiction professionals. He has also written *The Alcoholism and Drug Abuse Patient Workbook* (2003c) and the *Gambling Addiction Patient Workbook* (2003b). These workbooks have all of the exercises patients need to enter a stable recovery. His book entitled *Treating Alcoholism: How to Help Your Clients Enter Recovery* (2004) trains professionals how to treat patients with alcohol problems. He is the author of the book *God Talks to You* (2000) and the meditation tape *A Communication from God* (2008) by cdbaby, which help addicts make their first conscious contact with a Higher Power of their own understanding. He is a composer and has completed his second CD, *Peace Will Come*, music that helps addicts learn the essentials of a spiritual journey. With Dr. Jean LaCour (2004), he wrote the *Faith-Based Addiction Curriculum* to teach professionals of faith how to treat addiction. Dr. Perkinson is an international motivational speaker and regular contributor to numerous professional journals. He is the webmaster of several web pages, including www .robertperkinson.com, www.alcoholismtreatment.org, and www.godtalkstoyou.com, where he gets over 2.6 million hits a year and answers questions on addiction for free. His biographies can be found in *Who's Who in America, Who's Who in Medicine and Healthcare, Who's Who in Science and Engineering,* and *Who's Who in the World.*